Yee-Haw!

Galloping Through Horse World —A Wisdom Memoir

Nelson P. Miller

Yee-haw! Galloping through horse world—a wisdom memoir.

Miller, Nelson P.

Published by:

Crown Management LLC – May 2018

1527 Pineridge Drive
Grand Haven, MI 49417
USA

ISBN-13: 978-1-7322387-0-1

All Rights Reserved
© 2018 Nelson P. Miller
c/o 111 Commerce Avenue S.W.
Grand Rapids, MI 49503
(616) 560-0632
millern57@gmail.com

For Anne and Boo.
Love you two!

Table of Contents

Prologue		1
1	Breeds	3
2	Horses	8
3	Dogs	18
4	Training	25
5	Tack	39
6	Trainers	49
7	Owners	59
8	Breeders	68
9	Grooms	76
10	Grooming	83
11	Feeding	92
12	Family	99
13	Farms	105
14	Shows	114
15	Judges	123
16	Transport	133
17	Farriers	144
18	Vets	151
19	Loss	158
20	Talent	162
Epilogue		166

Prologue

The world is at once bizarre, broken, corrupt, and chaotic, while at the same time revealing flashes of exquisite beauty hinting of timeless order. Reflecting the broken world in which we live, I too am wretched, pitiful, poor, blind, and naked, yet simultaneously an image and child of God, of inestimable value, as are you. That profound tension between the corrupt and pure, obscene and stunning, and temporary and eternal, is the compelling story of my youthful gallop through horse world, of which this account is a light and one hopes somewhat humorous and insightful memoir. I hope that you find the horse context interesting. They are phenomenal animals, next to us undoubtedly God's greatest creatures, as his own word intimates. While dogs are humankind's best companions, intimate readers of our confused souls, horses evoke in us different attributes. Dogs and cats won't tell you your destiny, while horses will. Horses have the largest eye of any land mammal for a reason, not just to prepare for instinctual flight but also to mirror your spirit, foretelling your future.

Life gave me hard-earned and just grounds to write this book. For roughly ten years I worked full-time as a horse trainer, before moving on to a sensible career as a lawyer and law professor, where I've been for thirty years. Horse world, though, did something for me that a respectable career in law or any other responsible profession probably couldn't do. Horse world introduced me not just to odd men and women of towering talents and peculiar ambitions, or perhaps better put as peculiar talents and towering ambitions, but also to rapturously elegant and magically powerful animals. The unusual pursuit also offered me endless but somehow vitalizing physical labors, while introducing me to my wondrous wife who after my Lord will always be the biggest part of my story. She and I did most of horse world together.

Horse world taught me to work far harder and longer than I previously thought, or anyone sensible would have thought, possible. We are beings of boundless energy or, at least, boundless curiosity and abundant ambition, quick to recover from despairing exhaustion. Horse world, by the way, refers to one of those many peculiar American subcultures, perhaps like motorcycling, gardening, or sailing subcultures, but still quite different, as every American subculture is quite different. You may know another subculture. Horse world includes great variety from hunt clubs, racing for runners, trotters, and pacers, eventing, and dressage, to cutting horses, trail horses, pleasure horses, and show horses of many different breeds including the marvelous show ponies. Horse world is, admittedly, a privileged subculture, although truly, the privilege ends with the well to do who employ the unprivileged trainers or who send their worthy steeds to those trainers for monthly fees. Yet horse world also taught me that all striving is foolishness, meaningless, a wisp in the wind. Horse world teaches that beauty is at once everything, in the sense of a call to the eternal, and yet simultaneously nothing, ephemeral, gone in a glance. Horse world taught me that fortuities are not chance but handless design and yet also that human design has no chance. We are beings beyond our own design.

I waited thirty years to write this memoir, for a couple of reasons. One is that I had to learn to write, which is to process seemingly unconnected thoughts and experiences to express the hidden order that they always had. Writing is storytelling, and an author can't write until being able to discern the theme and movements of the story. The other and much better reason I waited until now to write about a horse-world past is that my wife finally asked. We rarely speak about our horse past, but when we do reminisce, we do so with a remarkably rich mix of emotions, from humor and awe to deep pain and loss, and then always to faith with a look forward to heavenly reunion. My wife and I know that heaven will include our favorite horses—and then again maybe some of our not-so-favorite horses but in fully redeemed and utterly enjoyable form. Now was simply the time to capture that turning from distant past to fast-approaching future. Enjoy.

1

Breeds

One of the most-obviously wondrous aspects of horses, something that non-horse people also readily recognize, is the pleasing variety of their breeds. Horses, of course, are domesticated animals, meaning that humans have been breeding them selectively for, well, millennia. Breeds have standards to which breeders attempt to conform. The standards sometimes depend on size (big for draft horses, small for ponies) or color (coppery gold with white manes for Palominos, spotted for Appaloosas), more often on features (arched necks, straight legs, angled shoulders, flat or muscled croups), and sometimes on a single performance capability, like how fast the Thoroughbred runs or smooth is the Tennessee Walker's riding gait.

Some breeds are ancient, like the Arabian horses whose bloodlines desert Bedouin tribes nurtured for long times. Other breeds are old, like some of the heavy draft-horse breeds emerging from medieval England and old Europe. Other breeds like the Thoroughbred arose with the dawn of modernity, while other breeds like the Morgan Horse are wholly modern creations, arising in that case from a celebrated progenitor stallion. They are all horses, even a child would readily recognize. Yet the breeds are so diverse and different as to take one's breath away. The massive Shire draft horse, standing over six feet at the withers, weighing up to a ton and a half, and with hooves larger than dinner plates, bears little resemblance to a dwarf miniature horse like Thumbelina, standing just seventeen inches and weighing about fifty-seven pounds. In the horse, God gave us such wonderfully malleable animals for husbandry.

Despite breed standards to which the animals should conform, a single breed can also offer substantial variety, with owners within the breed preferring one or another of their breed's strains. For instance, within the Arabian-horse breed, breeders preserve and develop Egyptian-bred Arabs, Polish-bred Arabs, and Spanish-bred Arabs, and lines from a single sire like the unparalleled Polish-bred sire Bask. While the Arab breed would maintain its overall standard, strains and lines would accentuate one or more of the breed's special characteristics, like the performance capabilities of Polish-bred Arabs, which the Poles bred for racing, or the fine heads and carriage of Egyptian-bred Arabs, which Egyptians bred not primarily for function like racing but instead more like art, to please and impress, for status, and as state gifts. Mares gestate a single foal for eleven months before birth, meaning that at most, a breeder gets just one chance at reproduction per year per mare. If you are impatient, then breed orchids or dogs, not horses. Because of the great expense of horse breeding and the long time breeding takes to have any significant influence, breeders tend to focus on one or another strain, line, or characteristic, so that Egyptian breeders may not even talk to Polish breeders. And so, horse world offers strain subcultures within breed subcultures.

If people disappeared from earth's face, leaving just their horses, then Saddlebreds would be the first to disappear after us. They wouldn't last much more than a day in the wild, with all the primping and pampering that these beautiful but relatively fragile horses require. Saddlebreds also don't have the reputation for being the smartest horses, bred instead for looks and performance function. My wife has a funny way of imitating a brainless Saddlebred looking for the comfort and security of the stable. When riding one, you kind of point it in any direction, and away it goes without any thought for the route or destination. Point it over a cliff, and it wouldn't even hesitate. Indeed, cuing a Saddlebred to change gaits or direction involves first getting its attention, awakening its pea-sized-seeming brain that a command is coming. Some breeds, like Arabs, do the thinking for you, too much so for the taste of many riders and trainers. They'll change gaits and directions six times before any command from their rider, which means riders must give constant attention to what their Arab steed is thinking about doing entirely on their own without any cuing or permission. Saddlebreds? Don't worry. Put yours in gear, and it pretty much stays there until you sound a trumpet fanfare that the next command is coming. That obliviousness to conditions is a large part of why they'd not last a day—maybe an hour—in the wild.

By contrast, the wizened mixed-breed horses that comprise a trail-riding stable would last far longer in the wild, already having managed to survive the brainless depredations of their amateur human mounts. Trail-riding horses must be smarter than their city-bred riders who, after all, know nothing about dangerous terrain, venomous snakes, or approaching severe weather. A good trail-riding horse is like a kind old woodsman uncle who takes you fishing when you've never been fishing. Among all the natural perils, you still get to relax in the hands of a master. Which breed, though, would last the longest without human care? The Przewalski's Horses, an ancient breed native to the Mongolian steppes that, unlike the wild horses on America's Western Plains or the Chincoteague ponies of the Maryland/Virginia shore, man had never domesticated. Indeed, the Przewalski's Horses would have been better without us. Still endangered, they were recently extinct in the wild until replenished from captured stock.

My wife and I were in Arab horses, or Arabians if you prefer. Among the many breeds, horse people know Arabs for their fine features and beautiful high-raised tails but also for their flighty nature. A trail-horse guide, the manager of a public riding stable, or an Amish family needing a trustworthy horse with which to buggy to market wants nothing to do with an Arab. An Arab would skitter off the trail and over the cliff-side at the crack of twig, or jump sideways ten feet at a shadow, dumping its public-stable rider, or dodge in front of an oncoming car at the flush of a roadside bird, endangering the Amish family. The Arab's skittishness is much of what endears it to the breed's owners. Turn an Arab loose in a ring to playfully shake an empty bleach bottle filled with stones at it, and you'll have a real tail-over-the-back, snorting, blowing, two-minute show out of it. When so animated, which one does easily with Arabs, the horses enchant with their floating, swirling beauty. Arab owners know that they share something special precisely because the horses are so sensitive to their surroundings and stimuli.

Indeed, Arabs are the forerunner hot-blooded horse, brought out of the Middle Eastern deserts to breed in England with larger and slower cold-blooded stock to produce the racing and jumping Thoroughbred.

This story is no myth or mystery but instead well-documented historical fact. Histories of the great Thoroughbred breed, the horses you see run at the Kentucky Derby every year, had long traced their lineage to three hot-blooded stallions imported in the early 1700s from Turkey, Syria, and Persia. Histories identified the three as the Byerley Turk, Godolphin Arabian, and Darley Arabian, each named for the English families that imported them and believed to be the dominant three sires out of a couple hundred other stallions imported from the same region. Yet recent DNA testing has identified offspring of the Darley Arabian as comprising ninety-five percent of the prevailing preferred Thoroughbred stock, meaning that the Darley's offspring ran away with the competition. Thomas Darley made a good bet when he bought the Darley Arabian, a 15-hand-high bay with a small blaze and three socks, in Aleppo, Syria, in 1704, to bring to England as a gift for his father. Hot-blooded Arabs mixed well with cold-blooded English stock, if racehorses were your thing. Like the Arab and other breeds, the Thoroughbred breed today has its own registry, ensuring the breed's purity while also ensuring things like unique names.

When I say that my wife and I were in Arabs, it happens that way, people falling into a breed and remaining there. Just as horse breeds remain pure and distinct, horse world permits surprisingly little crossover of people from breed circle to breed circle. Basic care and breeding, and then racing, showing, or other pursuits with these consumptive animals takes such incredible energy and substantial resources that one cannot manage making a name and having influence in more than one breed. Racehorse trainers, jockeys, owners, and grooms are just that—racehorse devotees and nothing else. They do not dabble on the side in Arabs or Appaloosas, or Pintos or Quarter Horses. Owners and trainers from different breeds may come together periodically for shows at annual state fairs, but even then, each breed concentrates its competition in a select few days. Some breeds tend to clump together at such events, like Arabs and Morgan Horses, so that Arab folks might get to know a few Morgan folks, especially the playful children and teens. But generally, people within one breed know nearly everyone in that breed in the same region of the country and no one much in any other breed.

So, for better or worse, my wife and I were Arab people. A family friend who was into jumpers once got me flying over jumps on a seventeen-hand Thoroughbred when I had no idea what I was doing, just to see if I took to it. I didn't. The leaps look and feel a lot bigger from the back of the mount than they do from the grandstand. Another acquaintance who was looking for a jockey once had me take a racehorse at speed once around the track to see if the speed attracted me. It didn't. One has far less control and feels far more vulnerable perched high and delicately on the back of a horse making a mad dash. I also once got to ride a good cutting horse as it separated out and headed off a frisky calf, but cow dung has a much worse consistency and very less tolerable smell than horse manure, and cattle just never made any sense to me. My wife had similarly brief experiences with jumpers and other breeds, but we stuck with Arabians.

The breeds tend to appeal to different demographics, although with many exceptions. Quarter-Horse people might think Arab owners to be rich and snooty, but Arab owners might think the same of Saddlebred owners and Saddlebred owners the same of Thoroughbred owners. Certainly, professional training to run your auction-bought Thoroughbred in a major race or have your dandied Saddlebred compete at a major show costs a lot more than taking your home-schooled Quarter Horse to the 4H fair. But Quarter Horses also have their high-stakes competitions, the horse stock and training for which may have high cost and thus require high owner income. Every breed has its hoity-toity trainers and owners but also its humble do-it-yourselfers. Horse people know who's special and who's not, or who *thinks* they're special and *knows* they're not, just like people do in other subcultures. You could be into barrel racing, occurring mostly among rural youth at small fairs, and you'd still recognize the glamorous royalty. Indeed, the healthy mix of rich and poor, educated and uneducated, privileged and unprivileged, is one of horse world's greater graces. The fifty-year-old broken-down groom stands at the same rail next to the billionaire owner, waiting for the winning or losing steed to race home. Rich and poor share in the excitement and satisfaction of the wins and pain and disappointment of the losses. God makes the same rain fall on everyone and made the unknown in us for him.

2

Horses

Horse people will tell you that the sport is all about how special certain individual horses are, sometimes ones that they have seen and appreciated from afar but also sometimes ones that they have owned and enjoyed in relationships that approach a curious sort of inter-species intimacy. Now, about this premise, I am unsure: the horses may not be special in themselves. If no one was around to breed, own, watch, train, ride, race, show, and appreciate them, then maybe the horses would be just another ordinary natural object. What may instead be special is the connection of horse to person. Some horses just seem made for their owner. You know how people sometimes say that dogs look like their owners (or owners like their dogs)? Well, horses and their owners don't look like one another, God forbid, but they do seem to have something of the same character or spirit sometime. You may even know some of the stories, like Penny Tweedy and her incredible, race-record-breaking Secretariat, although the stories don't have to be well-known to be special.

I could give you any of dozens of small, private examples. I once broke and trained a gelding that I initially thought incorrigible, worthless. He had such high energy, so little sense, so little confidence, and such an insensitive thickness about him, and was so ugly in face and color, had such a high cold back, and had such an ungainly gait, that I honestly thought that spending any money on training him was an abject waste—and the owner was paying *me* to train him. When I first mounted and rode him, his only gait was a dead run (gallop is the correct terminology). At his owner's insistence, we even *broke him to drive*, which at the time felt like an invitation to catastrophe. Asking any Arabian horse to tow a fragile-but-expensive four-wheeled buggy around behind it, among a sea of other Arab-towed fragile four-wheeled buggies, is indeed lunacy, especially when the buggies themselves sometimes fail catastrophically. Buggy wrecks, sometimes with serious horse, driver, or onlooker injuries, are relatively common at Arab shows. One loose-screw horse gallivanting its chattering buggy around the ring is enough to make several other horses loony, about which we'll see more later.

Yet in retrospect, breaking this gelding to drive turned out to be the best thing to tame his lunacy. The only reasonably safe way to break an especially flighty, mean, or sensitive horse to drive is to first teach it to pull a stone boat. A stone boat is just a small piece of plywood on low wooden runners on which a trainer can stand or, if the trainer doesn't trust the trainer's own balance, then pile stones. Put the leather breast piece on the horse, hook the breast piece's long leather traces to a short metal pipe attached by short ropes to the stone boat, and run the long driving reins from the bit and bridle through the surcingle's rings back to your hands. A *cluck* for giddy-up, *whoa* for stop, and use of the reins to turn and slow the horse gives the trainer a fighting chance at standing on the stone boat for the horse to pull the trainer along. You can't just stand on the stone boat and say *giddyup*. The horse will try taking one step and, feeling the resistance, stop and give up. You must instead hop on and off the stone boat until the horse gets the hang of leaning into the breast piece and pulling. The arrangement avoids the hazard of the horse kicking or otherwise destroying a perfectly good and quite-expensive buggy. Importantly, no fragile-wooden or solid-metal buggy shafts constrain, tickle, or offend the novice horse's sensitive sides, only the flexible leather traces. An adept trainer familiar with a stone boat can break to drive even buggy-destroyer horses, which I managed to do with several such intransigent horses sent to me especially for that purpose.

In this case, the ugly loony gelding took right to the stone boat. Pulling the weight of a trainer on wooden skids through the arena's soft dirt takes substantial strength and concerted effort. Yet the loony gelding inexplicably loved the focused effort of straining against the breast piece, as if he finally had a positive place to expend his unbounded energy. Concluding a strenuous workout with the stone boat, the gelding would literally lick his too-generous and too-floppy lips, heave a satisfied sigh, and hang his head in rest, eyes half closed in dream-like peace, a relaxed attitude and posture previously impossible for him. The stone-boat work somehow simultaneously strengthened and relaxed the gelding under saddle. Instead of careening about the arena at an ungainly gallop, he caught his balance and, within days, was able to canter respectably. In fact, I was quickly able to draw him back so slow in hand that a person could nearly keep pace at a brisk walk beside him as he gaily cantered. I was dumbfounded, although not convinced, especially insofar as his owner only left him for a month or two before taking him home. Yet, that summer and following summers, the gelding and his owner were regular *and successful* competitors, riding and driving. The owner even won costume classes—yes, dozens of Arab horses galloping around the ring all at once in flowing sequined regalia— with the gelding. God had made owner and horse for one another and no other.

My wife and I had our own favorites. Her favorite was easily Sam. I can't recall Sam's registered name. Breeders typically name their Arab horses with the stable name followed by the unique identifier, sometimes familiar English words or proper nouns, other times Arab, Egyptian, Polish, Spanish, or other foreign-sounding names. For an example of the latter, my family once owned and I trained and showed a gelding with the registered name *Cedardell Zzyzx*. Cedardell was a breeding farm whose owner had tired of naming horses, tired of breeders choosing unpronounceable names, and been amused at advertisers' efforts to be first in alphabetical listings with names like *AAA Auto Mechanics*, and so came up with the relatively unpronounceable but still-amusing name Zzyzx. The name gave fits to show announcers who would begin, "And in second place, Cedardell..." and then trail off into mumbling. Owners and trainers thus give their horses nicknames. Owners and trainers, though, sometimes don't use the same nicknames. Owners who needn't make their horses do anything generally don't have to deal with the more-difficult attributes of their horses with which trainers deal in trying to get the horse to do something useful. Trainers thus give some horses less-than-kind nicknames. A trainer might, for instance, ask a groom to "go saddle knucklehead" or "give dimwit an extra scoop of grain," and the groom would know exactly whom the trainer meant, even though the owner called the horse *Darling* or *Sweetie Pie*.

My wife had good reason to love Sam. He was one special horse, although initially his quality was not obvious. We couldn't have afforded him if he had obvious talent. Shoot, we couldn't afford him as it was, but we bought him at an unreasonably low price from a great couple for whom we trained several other horses. They honestly just wanted Sam to have a good home and sold him to us for far less than he was worth. Sam came out of a pig pasture—that was a *pig* pasture, not a *big* pasture. Honest. My wife says I exaggerate this one, but I don't. His breeders, this great couple, raised and sold hogs, among other employment, pastimes, and businesses. The hogs had the run of the place. The valuable breeding and show horses had their own pasture and stalls, with the best of the horses off with the trainer. The kindly, big-galumph gelding Sam, no part of the farm's breeding program, had to run with the hogs. Sam's lack of place in anyone's plans was another reason we got him for a song. My wife and I were a very young couple of no means, with precious little savings, and living largely month to month solely on training fees net of significant training expenses. Nonetheless, buying the right horse at the right price for a bit of training and a quick flip could be financially smart. Moreover, I knew that in a public-training-stable business where the hard and unending work was all about the clients and their horses, my precious young wife needed her own place and identity, which meant that she needed her own horse.

Amusingly, Sam had a couple of attributes that made me question whether we were getting the bargain that my wife thought, even though she had no question that Sam was the right horse. First, Sam had big, floppy ears, something you don't see that often on a horse—definitely a mule (half horse, half donkey) but not a horse. When Sam walked, jogged, or cantered, his big ears would flop back and forth in time with the cadence, which is not a sharp look for a horse. Second, Sam had an easy back, nearly a sway back, which again is not a good look for a horse. You usually see sway backs only on very old horses. Sam was a young horse, but he had a definite settling of his spine between the withers at the fore and croup at the rear. Floppy ears and sway back concerned me but not my dear wife. And no surprise, she turned out to be entirely right. With better food, rest, training, and fitness, and something challenging and interesting to do with his formerly useless life, Sam made a big turnabout. His ears stopped flopping, most of the time, at least. And his easy back tightened up a little while remaining easy enough to take a saddle smartly. Riding Sam, you felt like you fitted right in, with his great long arched neck rising high above you, and his strong flat croup well above you to the rear.

Sam was the best-natured, most-willing horse with which I ever worked. He had not a mean or anxious bone in his body. Dogs could chase him and swing on his tail in the paddock, and yet he would just play along and wouldn't even kick because he knew it was their game. If his rider lost a stirrup or dropped a rein, then he'd gently stop until the rider was right again. One day, my wife suggested that we break Sam to drive. It didn't take any breaking, not even the stone boat. I just slipped the buggy's hard and cold shafts up alongside him, confirmed that they didn't disturb his sensitive ribs in the least, and off we went driving, and not just in the ring but down the road outside. I drove Sam over to the farmhouse across the street where my wife and I lived and, to her astonishment, hollered at her to come outside and take her horse Sam for a drive. My wife loved Sam and did more than her share of winning blue ribbons with him in English, Western, sidesaddle, and halter.

Wisely, we later bought, trained, showed, and even bred Sam's full sister Chantelle. We called her *Shani*. Shani, too, was special but in a different way than Sam. If Sam was hidden but reliable talent, then Shani was *hot* talent, not just a performance and halter winner but also performance and halter *champion* in the right hands, which just happened not to be my wife's skilled hands. As well as my wife did with Sam, she couldn't quite do with his sister Shani. Shani was a pistol who under saddle took both a firm intention but light hand. She was so talented that she could swap leads (a difficult flying lead change) at a whim, which Shani would do repeatedly against my wife's wishes in the middle of a class with my wife riding her. No ribbon. Shani would also do a little jig with my wife instead of walk, another no-ribbon misstep. You had to kind of get Shani walking and then just trust her to keep doing so (a mysterious thing that I just couldn't adequately explain to my wife) rather than hold her up tight, which would just encourage her to jig. I loved showing her—hot talent that got rider and horse noticed—for the same reasons that my wife didn't. Poignantly, we sold Shani just as we left the farm to go off to law school. The money that we got for Shani, from a Florida breeder who would send her for breeding to a top national stallion, paid for my first year of law school. I doubt that any of my classmates paid their way partway through law school on horse money like I did.

My wife, who has an eye for animals, picked out another extraordinarily special horse when she discovered Bert. Bert wasn't his name, of course. My wife found him running in and out of foot-deep muck in the bottom of an old barn with a few cows, at a way-off-the-beaten path place in a small town of which no horse person had ever heard. The gelding's name at the time was Avatar Antares, first for a stable by that name and then, I gather, for a red-giant star in the Scorpius constellation. Bert was around eight years old at an absolute dead end in horse life, having literally broken the back, we were told, of his previous owner/rider in falling backward over on her in a final fit of incorrigibility. Yet despite the frank warning, and apparently confident that her young trainer husband could handle the risk, my wife could only see how high the gelding stepped with a natural action unseen among Arabian horses. I thought that the gelding's high-stepping action was due to the foot-deep cow muck. We arranged to buy him for the price of horse meat. He was so extremely flighty, spooked at the least unexpected sound or movement, eyes wide and nearly rolling back in his heard, that my wife nicknamed him Bert after the nutty father character on the old sitcom soap-opera spoof *Soap*. The name fit his looks and character perfectly.

Bert, though, turned out to be the most-talented and valuable horse that we ever trained, no less owned. My wife and I paid for only half of Bert, which was all that we could afford, even though, as I said, he came at the cheap price of slaughter meat. My parents paid the other half until my wife and I moved to another farm. We then found a kindly elderly couple to buy my parents' half of Bert so that their grandson could someday ride him, if I managed to settle Bert down into some semblance of reliability. We kept the other half. Bert was unquestionably a long-term project, given his extreme distrust of humans and abject fear of just about anything. On the other hand, he wasn't mean or even that obstinate, just a total nut case about everything. And I didn't find him that dangerous to ride, either. To keep him from rearing up and backward, you just had to stay out of his mouth, treating him lightly in keeping with his extreme sensitivity. And then you just had to manage to stay on his back, which was a little humped and cold rather than deep, warm, and easy. With his slightly humped back, extreme athleticism, and wild response to any stimuli, staying on Bert was a bit like riding a sledding saucer upside down, as he shifted speeds, gaits, and directions frantically at any shadow.

Yet as is often true of things, what makes for the greatest challenge also makes for the greatest opportunity. Bert's extreme sensitivity and wild gait ultimately made him the highest-stepping Arabian horse ever shown, a five-time National Champion in park, formal driving, combination, and amateur, although those victories went to others' credit. Instead, I spent a couple of long years coaxing Bert through hundreds of hours of training exercises, including patient ground working, steadying dressage movements, and long, settling and soothing trail rides. The patient work eventually lead to spectacular debuts at local and regional shows. I remember other trainers coming to ringside just to see Bert enter. Our elderly partners then bought out my wife and I when, in truth, we could no longer afford his catapulting value. They turned around a short while later and sold Bert to the nation's leading performance trainer for far more money. After making him a National Champion, that trainer then sold Bert to an airline executive for far more money than an Arab gelding or performance horse had ever sold, several hundred times what my wife and I had originally paid for him. My wife and I happened to dine with that trainer and his wife years later, giving us the chance to tell them the story of how my wife discovered Bert. I don't think that they believed us. Bert absolutely enthralled my wife and I, and not just for his extreme gait but for the extreme trust that he gradually developed in us and his extreme sensitivity. You'll never see a larger, softer, wilder eye on a horse anywhere, as if, indeed, God drew his spirit from a red-giant star in a far-off constellation.

While my wife was a master at spotting animal talent, I had one good horse that predated her. Elixir was a sixteen-hand, spooky, dark-liver-chestnut, three-year-old gelding when my parents bought him for me when I was sixteen. Elixir came along at just the right time, when I wasn't training for a living yet but instead apprenticing with one of the nation's top trainers. I was spending four hours every day working the trainer's horses at his farm, under his sharp eye. Generously, the trainer let me board and train Elixir at his farm, also under his sharp eye. With the trainer's guidance and the benefits of his first-class facility, Elixir got so fit, strong, and well-schooled that he won everything that a gelding ridden by a youth amateur could win. After winning many local and regional championships in English, Western, amateur, and halter competition, we traveled to Albuquerque at year end where we won Reserve National Champion in the English performance division. I even won a stock-horse equitation class with him and competed in that division, too, at the National Championships, which almost cost me the English-division reserve win. Elixir got so spooked and jumpy doing the stock-horse slides and spins that he bobbled once in the English division final.

The special thing about Elixir, though, wasn't his competition wins. He could do things that no other horse I ever trained could do. The trainer under whom I worked would occasionally travel somewhere across the country to do a training demonstration. Because he didn't always have a horse of his own at the peak of its performance, or at least one that he was willing to haul across the country just to show off in a public demonstration, the trainer took Elixir and me. My role was the groom, of course, not the demonstrator, although sometimes he'd put me on Elixir to demonstrate something while he explained it over a microphone to the assembled crowd. Riding and talking to a crowd at the same time can be a little hard, although the trainer was usually well up to it. Most often, though, he'd ride Elixir around showing off the fancy things that few horses can do, not just two tracks at all gaits and simple figure-eight flying-lead changes but also pirouettes at a canter, piaffes, passages, and lead changes *every stride,* a most-difficult series of maneuvers that makes the horse dance across the ring. Elixir could also do tricks, like a circus bow (forelegs stretched out front, head tucked between them, with a deep bow until the forelegs' elbows nearly touch the ground) with a rider on, kneel with rider on, rear and stand on his hindlegs with rider on, and Spanish walk, which involves raising each front leg artificially high in a sort of goose-step action. Elixir would also lay down at the rider's command, so that the rider could step right off onto the ground. When the rider was ready to get back on, you'd only have to mount Elixir on the ground and tell him to get back up. Oh, and he would nod *yes* or shake his head *no* on a command so subtle that most could not detect it, making it look like he was answering your questions.

Elixir was, in short, amazing. After a couple of years of winning everything one could win and doing everything one could do with a horse, I moved on to training others' horses, literally putting Elixir out to pasture, letting his glistening dark show coat fade in the sun. He'd earned the break, standing out in the pasture among the mares, covered in thick mud. A couple years later a wealthy West Coast client, a kind and fun family man who owned a long string of Burger King outlets, was looking for a top horse for his teenage daughter, and my parents sold Elixir to him. After Elixir got out to the San Francisco area by commercial van, the client flew me out to show his daughter what Elixir could do. The experience was poignant, like introducing one's best friend to an acquaintance whom you knew would become their new best friend, when you would never see your old best friend again. And the teen did become Elixir's new best friend, getting Elixir back into shape on her own before winning everything on the West Coast and beyond that a teen could win with a talented Arab gelding. She and her family had much the same experience that my family and I had with Elixir, as the teen grew in maturity, skill, and confidence, pouring her energies and talents into a beautiful sport while many of her peers lacked similar opportunities. Elixir got to raise two families, not just one, the gentlest, most-talented giant of an Arabian horse with a heart made for nurturing the confidence of a youthful companion. Heaven has a special place for him carrying the precious children of God.

I never came close to having another horse so well trained to do so many hard and impressive things so easily, although I sure tried. Training clients don't just give their horses to you for years to teach their horse everything that you know. You get their horse for a month, three months, maybe six or nine months if very fortunate, and then the horse goes back to the owner to save the monthly training fee and for the owner to ride and enjoy. For the trainers, most years start with all or nearly all new horses. Training is thus working constantly with green and up-and-coming horses, seldom if ever with trusty veteran horses, especially if you are a young and only modestly skilled trainer from whom older, better-known, more-established trainers rightfully poach horse-training clients and their talented up-and-coming horses. Getting to work so steadily and effectively with Elixir, and having so much success with him, was a great gift to me. Yet that success also haunted me in the difficult ensuing years, as I learned the hard way that I'd never achieve similar success, surely never again have a horse with which I could do and share so much, and to which I could grow so close. Indeed, for every golden horse, a trainer may deal with dozens of ordinary, and quite a few tough, customers. I'll spare you any examples here. Let's remember the good ones together. Avoid the noise of life, while seeing God alone in place of the world's insufficiency.

3

Dogs

Yes, this book is about horses, but pause just a moment to appreciate the role that dogs play in horse world. Horse world wouldn't be the same without them. Nearly every horse farm has farm dogs. The farm dogs vary as widely as do the horses. The dogs have no formal role. They are not part of the productive equation. They don't tend the horses, for instance, instead more so annoy them. A few dogs may serve as guards or sentries, alerting their human owners and keepers by bark or whine to thieves or other trespassers, not to mention loose horses whose paddock gates or stall doors happen to come open in the middle of the night. Dogs may also discourage pigeons, crows, possum, racoons, rats, and other fowl and vermin that can tear at feed bags and soil the lofts and rafters. Yet most farm dogs are more-or-less useless for those helpful sentry roles, too sound as sleepers and not sufficiently attuned to the wiles of their masters' foes. Farm dogs instead play an important *emotional* role, magnifying, clarifying, and reflecting the stable's spirit through the attention, frustration, and affection that their owners and keepers shower on them. A farm is not a farm until it has its defining master-to-dog relationships and roles.

The horse-whisperer trainer for whom I apprenticed, for instance, had bird dogs. When he wasn't breeding, training, and showing horses, which was nearly all the time, you could find him across the dirt road out back of the old barn where he kept a kennel of bird dogs. He wasn't a hunter. He just liked to be out in the country walking or riding with his English setters as they ran the old rock piles and bushy fence lines of the fallow fields. Breeding, training, and showing was intense. Following bird dogs through the beautiful countryside was pure escape, pastoral pleasure. If my mentor rode a horse to accompany the dogs rather than walked, then the mount was some scruffy old mare or gelding so that getting its leg tangled and scarred in old fence wire, or its ankle twisted and swollen in an old post hole, wouldn't matter. The athletic, spotted, shaggy, and exceedingly friendly dogs would run, bound, snuffle, and point, until they were tuckered out, the fun was over, and he haled them back to the old barn. The crazy-fun bird dogs, scruffy old careless horses, and free outdoor sporting activity reminded the trainer and, to a degree, his employer, clients, and apprentices of the natural relationship of man to domesticated animals, as working companions. One of the trainer's two sons kept Beagles, so that dad and son would occasionally run their different-breed dogs together, more than doubling the canine chaos and sporting fun. Man, those beagles could howl and run. Sometimes, they'd get so out of hand as to end up in the next county, located and retrieved days later by the proud son.

The trainer's other, older son liked Border Collies but kept Australian Shepherds, which was how my wife and I got into Aussies. I worked horses at the trainer's farm when the older son was still there, sometimes also working horses. The older son soon married, had a child, and moved away to run another horse farm. But before he did, we went around together to some dog breeders and shows, scouting Border Collies and Aussies. He bought a female Aussie whom everyone called Troubles for the havoc that she created back on the farm. Aussies naturally love to worry horse and cattle stock, meaning to make them move around field or paddock, and to turn and gather, which is the work for which breeders initially bred the dogs. Early each morning, when the farm hands would lead the spirited horses from their stalls out to paddocks, Troubles would bark at the horses' heels, aggravating them in gleeful anticipation, while the hands yelled at her to quit so that they could manage the leaping and twisting horses. As soon as the hand turned a horse loose in the paddock for it to dash off to dispel its pent-up energy, Troubles would snarl after it at top speed, urging it to run. When the fun of putting the horses out to paddock was over, and the horses had settled to munch hay in a shed or search for grass under the fence line, Troubles would try to stir up more fun by running up and down outside

Yee-Haw!

the paddock, yapping endlessly at the yawning horses, until someone howled at her to shut up. The routine was as predictable as sunrise.

I soon bought an Aussie we named Tut, from our veterinarian and, a while later at a dog show, an Aussie we named Ruby. Tut, a big blue merle, loved the farm. He'd follow us for miles when we went trail riding up and down the dirt roads that surrounded the farm. He was the easiest dog we ever had, ultimately too easy. Tut took to disappearing for days at time, which at first deeply concerned us but soon, after his many happy returns, troubled us only for the nocturnal havoc he might be causing with deer or other game, we hoped not with neighbors' livestock, although we heard rumor of him worrying some nearby sheep. With Tut's inexplicable frequent forays, Ruby, a small red tricolor, became the farm's mainstay dog. A cute bundle of happy and mischievous energy, Ruby was into everything and a part of everything, having a fear of missing out. If someone was in the arena working horses, then she was laying or ambling about the arena, cognizant but respectful of the energetic workout. If time came for a trail ride, then she was right at one's side. Feeding time was her favorite, though. As the feed cart approached each stall and the horses poked their big, soft muzzles out of the cut-out holes for the feed scoop, anticipating the rich grain-and-molasses mix, Ruby would jump up and nip the nose of any horse foolish enough not to see her sneaking up at them. You couldn't bend over to greet and pet Ruby without her jumping up in friendly excitement to poke you with her nose right in your eye. Mention Ruby to this day to my wife, and she'll scrunch up one side of her face as if to rub a dog-poked-sore eye.

While Ruby loved nipping the horses' noses at their feed boxes and chasing them in their paddocks, trying to catch and swing on their tails, she also loved making game of a small Norwich Terrier dog my parents owned, called Gator. After a long day at the barn, time came for the dogs to join us in walking the couple-hundred yards from the barn back to the house for dinner. Here, though, was another of Ruby's favorite moments. Ruby loved to pester Gator as he made his way home, trying to grab his short tail to lift his back end off the ground in play, especially if she could get him running, which was most days. Gator took to trying to sneak away from the barn a few minutes early before everyone else headed home. He'd tuck his short tail, duck his head, and quietly trot toward home with frequent glances back over his shoulder for Ruby's onslaught. Then, just when he'd thought he'd made it safely out of range, he'd start his dash for home, somehow always a little too late to avoid Ruby *and* a little too early to reach the safe haven of home. The barn was uphill from the house with a swale in the two-track driveway between them. From her high vantage at the barn, Ruby would see Gator streaking with his stubby little legs toward home, and she'd take off running at full speed, always in time to grab the disgusted Gator by the tail as he snarled, ran, and tumbled the rest of the way home. You've never seen a dog so satisfied at the end of a day as Ruby.

Ruby had other barn games that she loved to play, one of them priceless for its hilarity. My wife bought a miniature Shetland Sheepdog on the first month-long show trip that we took, together with two grooms and eight horses, to Florida right after we married. She called him *Blue*, short for his registered name Blueberry. A Sheltie breeder had brought him to one of the shows, and my wife fell head over heels for him. But Shelties, bred for small size and beautiful coats, are not necessarily that bright. Blue, a kennel-raised nine-month-old when we got him, was first extremely shy, second naïve in the extreme, and third just not very smart. His sale to my wife and introduction to our horse caravan so traumatized him that he sat for days doing nothing but drooling. Eventually, though, he got the hang of the farm and loved it, especially because of his revered ringleader Ruby. Ruby knew her status as Blue's champion and took full advantage of it. The best example, the hilarious one, was that whenever a cat crossed their paths, as they often did around the barn, Ruby would catch Blue's eye to induce him to follow her in a mad dash for it.

Cats have their own role in horse world but only as foils to dogs, as the coming story about dogs chasing cats well illustrates. Barn cats are a necessary evil, being effective at discouraging mice and rats from making a mess of the feed area but bringing their own needs and messes. That, by the way, is a farm's nature, one mess requiring another. Ruby and Blue, often joined in these escapades by the slower and smaller Gator, didn't want to catch a cat because they knew the claw wounds that would result. But if they could get the cat to run, which was often because the cats knew how to cooperate, then they trusted that a safe game was on. The barn in which this fun all occurred had a rectangular path that the chase could follow from one cement aisle of the barn to another aisle and back around again through another narrow hallway. The race would ensue, the cat leading the dog pack skittering round and round the four corners of the large rectangle... until the cat would discretely jump on top of some feed barrels just after it had raced around one corner ahead of the dogs and momentarily out of their sight. The dogs, oblivious to the cat's trick, would careen around the corner, racing past the feed barrels with the cat calmly looking down at them as they raced by, the dogs having assumed incorrectly that the cat had instead raced on ahead just around the next corner. The dogs would then make two or three more circuits around the rectangle in mad pursuit of a cat that they assumed was just around the next corner, when instead the cat sat atop the feed barrels watching with amusement as the dogs raced repeatedly by. No matter how many times the cat pulled the same trick, the game never grew old. My wife and I believe that Ruby knew exactly what was going on but just wanted to make more fun of it.

Blue would have been clueless without Ruby. Once again, shelties are so inbred for their small size and gorgeous Collie-like coats that they can be quite hairbrained. Blue, for instance, would only come in one door of the house. If Ruby happened to come in the back door instead of the front door to which Blue had accustomed himself, and Blue intended to follow, he would instead stand outside the back door bobbing and half-lunging as if to try to jump through the open back door until he would finally admit his inability and run around front. After many attempts at coaxing Blue through the back door, my wife finally gave up and would just tell him, *Go around front! Go around front!* to which he would dutifully obey, never able to come in the back door, even to follow in Ruby or another dog. Yikes. To Blue's credit, his inability to enter through the back door, a sliding door with a screen, may have had a little to do with his having bounced off the screen on one of his first attempts, but the real reason seemed instead to have something to do with his bred-in circling instincts that would cause him to run little circles whenever excited. Blue also spent a lot of time hiding or sleeping under the bed. *Where's Blue?* my wife would sometimes ask, as if she didn't know, when of course he was under the bed. I don't know about your bed, but ours had very little room under it. Blue would have to crawl on his belly to get under it, but under he'd go, often not to come out for hours at a time. My wife took to laying down beside the bed and dragging him out at times, to go for a ride, go outside, or eat.

Other than those and a few other odd things, Blue was a pretty good dog—hardy, for sure. He once found himself up in the loft of the barn when he saw Ruby having some fun in which he wanted to join down on the main barn floor. You could see his little mind working but only for a moment. Rather than run safely around the barn and down, he leapt the eight or ten feet straight to the barn floor, fortunately none the worse for the adventure. Ruby taught Blue to chase crows and other birds from off the tops of tall stacks of hay and straw bales out back of another stable where we worked. Ruby would bound up the stacked bales, the much-smaller Blue trying gamely to follow. Blue, though, had a habit none of the other dogs acquired. He'd sneak out at night to traipse a half-mile down the dirt road to stalk and fuss at a neighboring farmer's pigs throughout the night, coming back early in the morning looking drunk with the fun and smelling like pigs, whereupon he'd collapse somewhere to sleep it off until dinner. That fun was all his own, the other dogs never quite understanding.

Blue also once got completely lost. After days of hunting for him and even advertising for his return, we got a call from a nice family located a couple miles away saying that they had heard on a radio message board that we'd lost a dog fitting the description of the one that they'd found. My wife and I excitedly got in the car and headed over to the address that they gave us. When we rang the doorbell of the very nice new mini-mansion at the given address, a pert teen opened the door and politely invited us inside. There sat Blue, resting comfortably on a special blanket on the handsome father's lap, the father sitting in a big leather easy chair facing a crackling fire in the great stone fireplace of the mansion's sumptuous living room. A perfect family, including petite blond mother in an apron and two other well-dressed children like the one who had greeted us so kindly at the door, sat arrayed happily around the living room. Blue looked at us, as if to say, *I don't know these people—what are they doing here?* He looked so at ease that I thought of nudging my wife and whispering to her to deny that Blue was hers so that he could stay. He'd never looked that confident at our home. But too late. My wife was already rejoicing at Blue's discovery and coming return. Not only Blue, but also the family, looked disappointed.

My wife had a soft spot for dogs but, at least then, not quite the eye that she had for horses. Otis was another case in point. At that same first string of shows in Florida to which we went just after marrying, when my wife got Blue, we also briefly had Otis. My wife had disappeared with the two grooms for an hour, I had no idea where, until they came back from the dog pound with Otis. This foray was one that I little understood. We were at a fairground in a sketchy part of the large and unfamiliar metropolitan Tampa area, having just come up from showing at a racetrack in Miami. We already had more animals on our hands than we could reasonably handle, including three difficult stallions. We were undermanned, underfunded, exhausted, and about fifteen-hundred miles from home. We also had one last show for which to prepare, where we needed to do well to justify what had already been an expensive, risky, and arduous trip. And here across the fairground from the parking area came my wife, the two grooms, and a great big Saint Bernard dog whom they introduced to me as Otis, rescued from the dog pound. The industrious grooms, whose boundless energy and good spirits saved the trip for us, immediately took to bathing, grooming, and walking Otis, as if he were just another one of the eight horses. He only stayed a few days with us, if I recall correctly, before they took him back to the pound or maybe found another home for him. Whatever his end, Otis sure had a few days of the good life. Stable dogs have it made, while helping make it for us, their intimacy respecting our own solitude.

4

Training

Training is a stable's lifeblood. Training makes turnips into spring salad, stones into savory soup. Training is the value-add that lends a worthless horse worth, giving a useless horse a meaningful role, not only a job but sometimes even a ministry. Training can rescue the devil's horse from the slaughterhouse, just as it elevates the average horse to good, good horse to great, and great horse to superstar. Training turns a pasture horse into a halter horse, halter horse into pleasure-riding horse, pleasure horse into performing horse, and performing horse into show, stock, driving, or circus horse. Training is hard labor, real work, methodical, gaining by increments, but it is also transformative, magic, a mystery, and profound, like walking into the barn one day to discover a new animal that training transformed. Training isn't a guarantee. Bad training can ruin a horse, turning a gentle mount into a frightened killer, a free spirit into a broken heap, in some cases even killing a horse through accident or stress. Good training, though, can do the opposite, saving a horse from the glue factory, redeeming a lost talent into a productive and even treasured horse.

I had lessons from various decent-or-better horsemen but didn't know the power and purpose of a top-notch trainer until apprenticing for one in my mid-teens. My trainer likely wouldn't have known the scientific theory behind his wizardry (he may not have completed high school), but he was nonetheless a master at what behaviorists would call *operant conditioning*. The clearest example was his skill at loading a horse in a trailer when the horse didn't want to load. While the feat may not seem like much, that one achievement of loading an intractable horse was the crowd favorite at any of his exhibitions. When he put on one of these exhibitions, to which I accompanied him on several occasions, we would take a horse or two of our own, usually one that I had fitted and schooled for him as he did the more-important things that famous trainers do, but that he had finished or otherwise knew well. Riding that horse, he would demonstrate difficult maneuvers that attendees had probably never seen before, like pirouettes at the canter, piaffe, passage, Spanish walk, and of course tricks like having the horse count, nod or shake its head in purported answer to silly questions, bow, kneel, and lay down. Few horses can do any tricks, no less so many entertaining ones. Many in the crowd would never have seen such things. But loading the intransigent horse was always the crowd favorite, while also by far the best illustration of operant conditioning.

To set it up, my mentor trainer would call ahead, telling the stable that hosted the exhibition to have available for his demonstration a horse that the stable could not load in a trailer, despite herculean effort. Every stable has at least one horse that is scared stiff of the trailer, which is basically a tin can into which you must stuff the horse before scaring it to death careening down the road. No wonder some horses don't take to getting into the trailer, especially one hauled by a person who doesn't understand how hairy the ride can be if one doesn't take corners, acceleration, and braking slowly. Horses hauled by insensitive drivers have good reason not to want to get into a trailer ever again. Trailers are plain scary for most any horse. Some horses must take sedatives not to go berserk inside of them, roaring seventy miles per hour down curvy, potholed, truck-packed highways. Making matters worse, the customary way of loading a horse is to walk it up to the trailer so that its head is pointed in and then to whip, shove, and holler at it until, a total basket case, the horse finally clamors in. The abuse of trying to force the horse into the trailer conditions the horse to despise the whole contraption, and rightly so, given that a sickening ride usually follows. Severe negative reinforcement is why every stable has a horse that no one can load, despite coordinated sweaty efforts of two, three, even four burly men locking arms and shoving the horse in.

This trainer, though, knew operant conditioning's power. He'd have the stable place the trailer in the center of the arena. A handler would then lead the recalcitrant horse into the arena, from which the crowd could instantly tell the problem, as the horse reared and pulled back to shy and frantically drag its handler away from the trailer. The crowd would *ooh* in appreciative alarm. My mentor trainer would invite the handler, indeed as many at once as wished to try together, to load the horse, of course to no avail despite the greatest effort and quite a bit of chaos. As soon as the effort proved obviously fruitless, even dangerous, the trainer would dismiss those who had tried. The trainer would then lead the horse *away from the trailer*, which was the first proper step in operant conditioning. Well away from the trailer, the trainer would lunge the horse in tight circles, making sure that the horse advanced at a brisk pace whenever the trainer clucked and cracked the whip over it, which the horse was initially relieved to do. What can be easier than gallivanting around and around in tight circles? ... except that the trainer was making the horse expend great energy dutifully complying with his simple commands. The only time that the trainer would stop the horse from its exhausting tight-circle gallivanting, indeed stop and *stroke the horse* like a best friend, loosen its tight halter, and maybe give it an apple, was when... the horse faced the trailer. The trainer had, in effect, switched the reinforcement. Now, instead of pain and punishment when approaching the trailer, the horse had multiple rewards.

But just as the horse recovered sufficiently to begin once again to consider the trailer, back the trainer would go to gallivanting the horse round and round in tight circles, except now the exhausting tight circles were getting gradually closer to the trailer. The trainer would then stop the horse again but with the horse now directly facing the back entrance to the trailer. More strokes and quiet words of encouragement ensued, as the horse quietly looked the trailer over like maybe now it was not such a bad thing, but then on command back the horse went to gallivanting exhaustingly, until another stop ensued even closer to the trailer. By now, the crowd could see the horse leaning toward the trailer, *wanting to get into the trailer* for the peace, rest, strokes, and apples that the trailer would surely supply. But *no!* the trainer wouldn't *let* the horse get in the trailer, until the horse did some more tight-circle gallivanting. But *no!* the horse *wanted* to get in the trailer for rest, the crowd would lean forward, as if to entreat the trainer with *don't you see*?! The crowd couldn't understand why the trainer wouldn't *let* the horse get in the trailer. *Let the horse get in!* the crowd would root and cheer. Until finally, the trainer would relent and, on one of the trailer rest stops, let the horse walk or even jump right in, without even a command to do so. The whole thing took five minutes, tops, sometimes even just two or three minutes. And the training more than stuck. Indeed, the funniest part came when the trainer would back the horse out of the trailer, but the horse would try to immediately jump right back in. The achievement seemed a miracle, especially considering that some of these exhibition horses hadn't been loaded in a trailer successfully for years.

My mentor trainer used the same operant conditioning when training trail horses. A trail class in an Arabian show is an anomaly, unusual, whereas the class would be common in a more-conventional Western breed like Quarter Horses, Pintos, Palominos, or Appaloosas. Arabs are showier, more suited to English and park classes. Arabs are also flightier, much less suited to trail classes. A trail class involves moving various odd obstacles that horse and rider might encounter on the trail, into the ring, where horse and rider must confidently negotiate each of them to impress the show judge. The obstacles typically include things like a short wooden faux bridge onto which the horse must step, inevitably making loud and scary *clump, clump* sounds with its shod hooves. Using the same technique that he used for loading a horse in a trailer, my trainer would within minutes have his horses running *for* the little faux bridge to stand joyfully atop it, rather than running *from* it as any excitable Arab would naturally do. Other trail-horse riders would stand their frightened mounts just short of the scary little bridge, trying to force the horse onto it using the rider's spurs and lashes from the long reins, conditioning the horse to greater fear and loathing of it. I loved using my mentor's proper conditioning technique to get just about any horse, confident or not, to clump proudly up onto the bridge that I built and kept near the arena just for the fun of it.

My horse-whisperer trainer had many other tricks up his sleeve, but his primary skill was observation. His upbringing with horses and the attention that he gave to their instincts, habits, fears, foes, and sensitivities, helped him see the subtlest things that no one else could see. He and I were once driving a pickup truck down a dirt road when we happened to come up behind a dog running along the roadside. *Watch,* he said, *that dog's going to run out in front of the truck.* The dog then surely did. *What did you see?* I asked him. *I don't know,* he replied, adding, *maybe something in its ears*. My mentor's observational skills served him well because horses, as prey animals rather than predators, are incredibly alert, picking up on the slightest environmental signals. Clever Hans, an especially sensitive trick horse of the early 1900s, proved the case. His trainer cued Hans so subtly that Hans, by tapping his hoof on the ground, appeared to be able to count, add, subtract, divide, do fractions, keep a calendar, and solve other problems. The trainer, an amateur and mystic, may not even have known that he was cuing Hans with subtle body language, depending on whether you judged the trainer a charlatan or fool. Horses pick up visual cues and tactile signals, like the slight movement of a finger of the trainer's hand laid comfortably across the horse's shoulder, which is an effective cue that humans do not readily see without keen observation, for amusing responses like counting with a fore hoof or nodding or shaking the head.

My trainer, no charlatan or fool, used, and other trainers use, operant conditioning's subtle association, generalization, discrimination, and reinforcement for more than tricks. Showing an Arabian horse at halter at the highest levels, like regional and national championships, requires that the horse come to the greatest alert attention at just the moment that the judge views it. The attention tends to hide the horse's conformation faults, perhaps a rounded rather than flat croup or a short and straight rather than long and arched neck, while also accentuating the horse's strengths, like fine head and straight legs. Believe me, I know. My learning the alert-attention techniques elevated my better halter horses from also-rans to regional champions and national competitors. Knowing the techniques means getting better horses from better horse-training clients. Clients know whether trainers have the skills to make a difference for their precious horses. Halter horses who come to full alert attention at the trainer's command in the ring are obvious next to those horses that do not for lack of their trainer's knowledge of the operant techniques.

By alert attention, I mean wide eyes riveted on the trainer, ears equally alert, frame drawn up on tiptoes, and tail high and muscles taut as if prepared for flight or attack. Here's where operant conditioning comes in. Back at the training stable, the trainer presents the horse with the alert cue, which in the show ring would be to gently raise the butt end of the whip from behind the back and up and over the trainer's head toward the horse's face and nose. The trainer or a helper then deploys the presenting stimuli with which they want the horse to associate the alert cue. A carbon-dioxide fire extinguisher, the kind that gives a loud puff of harmless white smoke, is one extremely effective presenting stimuli, although one could use a shimmery plastic bag, loud plastic bottle with rocks, large mirrors, or anything else that will catch the horse's attention. One puff of an extinguisher, though, will certainly get the horse's full attention. You must even be careful on the first puff that the horse does not take total flight, dragging away the helpless trainer. Operant conditioning done. In the show ring, the trainer need merely raise the butt end of the whip over the trainer's head toward the horse's nose—the associated cue to the loud puff of white smoke—and the horse comes to full alert looking for the offending fire extinguisher, which of course is stored safely in the barn. The association wears off quickly (behaviorists call the process *extinction*), but judicious use of the cue plus a rare reminder with the extinguisher back at the barn can preserve and restore the effect.

Some trainers eschew the extinguisher and use the whip itself. A whip, the most misunderstood of training tools by both trainer and lay person alike, can be effective when used to cue, stimulate, and guide a horse. To cue with a whip would be to do as just explained above, just showing the horse the whip to induce the horse into the associated behavior that the trainer desires and expects. To stimulate with a whip would be to pop it quietly or loudly in the air over the horse or tap the horse with it on the croup, neck, or flank without sting or welt, to call into play the horse's instinctual or trained flight reaction. To guide with the whip would be to point the whip low in front of the free or lunged horse to get it to stop, raise it in front of the free or lunged horse to get it to turn around, and raise it behind the free or lunged horse to get it to trot or canter forward. My trainer taught me to guide free horses in this manner using the whip while standing in the middle of a round ring, usually with the horse in a surcingle, bit and bridle, and side reins to help arch and shape the horse's neck and improve its carriage under saddle. Cuing free horses in this manner was also part of my trainer's exhibitions. My horse Elixir, whom I worked endlessly in this manner to fit him for a long summer show season, was especially good at responding to the whip's subtle cues. When we took Elixir to an exhibition, my trainer would turn him loose in the huge arena and then use nothing but the whip to direct Elixir all over the ring, walking, trotting, cantering, stopping, backing, turning, cantering off again, and ending with Elixir standing on his hind legs, again solely on whip cue, without a hand, rein, or lunge line on him, another exhibition favorite.

The problem with whips is that trainers and owners too easily use them to punish horses rather than cue, stimulate, and guide. Horses under training can frustrate and even anger anyone, even an otherwise-skilled trainer. Anger and frustration must not be the motive to employ a whip. A whip in the hand of a mean or out-of-control trainer is a destructive instrument, the painful lash and welts from which will turn a confused or recalcitrant horse into a mean-spirited man-hater. Properly deployed, a whip should never leave a mark or even a significant sting on a horse. Its purpose is to alert and stimulate a horse with a non-stinging tap, sharp pop in the air, or flat noise-making whap along a non-sensitive part of the horse's broadly muscled neck or rear hide, to momentarily spook and arrest the horse. The whip that leaves marks makes the horse burn in resentment of trainer, whip, and desired work. No matter how talented they may once have been, badly whipped horses are useless, ruined for halter because of their pinned-back ears, resentful squint, and annoyed swishing of their tails, and ruined for riding or driving because of their sullenness and refusal to strive other than to defeat the desires of their hated handler.

A large and handsome dapple-grey stallion named Syncopate reminded me of what I already knew about the proper use of whips. Syncopate's owner had sent him to several trainers to win halter championships, which the stallion handily did, earning himself significant breeding privileges. One or more of those handlers, though, had, in trying to ensure the horse's most-excited response at halter, unfortunately abused Syncopate to fear and hate the handler's whip. Of this unfortunate fact, the owner had duly warned me, when the owner sent Syncopate to me to break to drive. Syncopate was also a buggy destroyer, which was why the owner sent him to me to break to drive. Horses can destroy a buggy with one swift kick or any number of different twists and leans inside the fragile wooden shafts of a show cart, out of fear or resentment for the whole constraining contraption. Syncopate's owner, an accomplished breeder but amateur showman, wanted to drive Syncopate himself, of which the owner was perfectly capable but for the fact that Syncopate had generalized his hatred for whips and trainers into also hating the confining labors of pulling a buggy, more than one of which he had destroyed. The stallion didn't need any more halter wins. His breeding popularity had waned, as naturally happens, and so the owner figured he'd entrust his beloved champion to me to get Syncopate to drive happily, trustworthily, and submissively—a tall order.

Syncopate and I accomplished that feat more easily than I at first imagined possible. The aforesaid stone boat, a trick by the way of my horse-whisperer mentor, once again did its magic. With only the soft leather breast piece and its long leather traces barely confining him, plus the surcingle, long reins, and bridle to which he was already accustomed, the large, muscular, and energetic Syncopate took readily to dragging me smartly around the arena while I stood on the stone boat. He loved the positive and peacefully tiring labors, as these domesticated animals of burden generally do. Like their human masters, horses generally love to work, unless spoiled from doing so. Trainers had spoiled Syncopate from halter showing, which he hated in association with the abusive whip, but pulling a stone boat was just foreign enough and just fun enough for him to love it. After he and I gained our full confidence with the stone boat, with me running alongside of it and jumping on and off as Syncopate alternately leaned into and relaxed off the leather traces, the next step to the two-wheel training cart was easy. The taut leather traces pulling the trainer-weighted stone boat had accustomed Syncopate's formerly sensitive rib cage to the buggy's constraining metal shafts, so that he had no objection to my sliding the shafts up alongside him as we gently took together the first few steps. I did take one precaution, which was to have a running-W (another trick of my mentor trainer about which I tell more, later) the first time that I tried the buggy, but I had no need of deploying it.

Syncopate now loved to drive. He was soon back at his owner's farm, happily pulling his owner around the place in a two-wheel cart and, before long, doing the same at shows pulling the fancy and expensive four-wheel cart, no longer a buggy destroyer. But Syncopate still hated the abusive whip. That lesson Syncopate abruptly taught me shortly after our driving feat together, along with the lesson not to get too confident too quickly over any such feat. Flush from the confidence of achieving the driving so swiftly, I foolishly assumed that Syncopate had somehow also forgiven trainers for their prior abuse with the whip. Fully mindful of his owner's warning *never* to so much as *lift* a whip in front of Syncopate, I thought that I would nonetheless try doing so. His owner had asked me to show Syncopate at halter and under saddle in an upcoming show, expecting that I would do so sans whip, as Syncopate had taught his prior abusive handlers to do and his owner had triply warned me. I thought that I'd look a little timid or foolish without at least carrying a whip into the ring, and so I stood Syncopate up on the cement floor of the barn's hallway, stepped the six feet back to the end of the show halter's lead facing Syncopate as a trainer would do in showing at halter, and picked up a tiny riding whip (not even the long halter show whip) that I had laid on the floor behind me.

No sooner had I picked up the tiny whip and just barely started to draw it from behind me to show it to Syncopate for whatever reaction it might engender, when something happened so fast that I never had an instant to move a muscle. Syncopate had instantly lunged forward the six feet to try, mouth wide open, to grab my face and throat and tear them from me. Syncopate had tried to kill me. Fortunately, though, his shod hooves had slipped on the cement as he lunged instantly and violently forward, so that he was only able to grab... the top button off my shirt. If I had tried the same insanely stupid thing in the solid sand footing of the arena, which was just steps behind me and I had considered doing, then Syncopate easily would have reached, grabbed, and driven my face and throat into the ground in front of him, probably then kneeling over and mauling me, as stallions have been known to do with trainers or handlers under the worst of circumstances. A stallion had done exactly that to a horse-trainer friend of mine whose face bore the scars for the rest of her life, saved only by her husband getting a shotgun to promptly kill the savage stallion. Syncopate, though, caught nothing more than a button. The near miss startled us both so much that we just stood there staring down one another, him with his sides heaving in fury and me gently stepping back and laying down the tiny whip. Of course, I never raised a whip around him again, not even when showing him at halter. That evening, my wife asked me where was the button missing from my shirt. *You'll need to ask Syncopate* was my only answer.

Training, as anyone should imagine, is indeed a lot about using appropriate presenting stimuli, association, reinforcement, and reward, all involving aspects of operant conditioning. A simple example is teaching a halter horse to stretch its neck out to its full extent. Halter classes judging the horse's conformation reward long necks. Hence, the handler's job is to make the neck appear as long as it is. The handler stands four to six feet in front of the horse, raises above the handler's head the handler's right arm holding the lead, and pulls or snaps the lead until the horse holds its head high, tips its chin up, and stretches out its neck. This awkward position that essentially has the horse looking uselessly upward, rather than forward and out for predators from which to flee, is so unnatural for the horse that the trainer must develop it. Operant conditioning requires stimulating the horse with the arm-raised position (that which one wants the horse to associate with raising the head and stretching the neck), prompting the horse with the pull and snap on the lead chain, and then (the key) releasing the chain the instant the horse stretches its neck ever so slightly more than it previously did, combining the chain's release with verbal encouragement and appreciative pats on the horse's neck. The rewards (positive voice and pats, and removal of the negative chain tension), timely and consistently applied, can teach any horse to stretch its neck to full extent.

Chaining and sequencing the neck stretch with the horse's other necessary operant performances, like posing the legs just right, standing stock still, and tensing to full attention with ears up, makes for the full performance. Trainers thoughtfully break down these complex performances into their constituent parts and train for each part before reassembling them into the full performance. Yet training is also about strengthening the horse to be able to perform as skilled operant conditioning hopes to induce. Physical strengthening is much more necessary for performance horses than halter horses, especially for the high-stepping action required of English and park horses under saddle, not to mention for the athletic maneuvers of stock horses, dressage horses, cutting horses, jumpers, and other performance horses. Trainers strengthen horses using special facilities like swimming pools, special equipment like treadmills and cavalletti, mechanical means like a running W or rubber hosing attached to cuffs at the foreleg ankles, stimulation like light chains or wooden rattles around the ankles, or long hooves and weighted shoes like Saddlebred trainers use. Mechanical training can produce high action of a type, but the action only raises the horse's legs in an obviously artificial manner, not elevating the horse itself, rider and all. Movement that mechanical means produce looks mechanical rather than athletic.

My trainer, though, the master under whom I apprenticed, had a more-natural and more-satisfying way, although also more-painstaking way, of producing high action out of pure athleticism, minus the mechanics. His method was the classical Haute Ecole used in places like Vienna's Spanish Riding School stretching back hundreds of years, also used among outstanding circus trainers of a more-recent age. The method takes full advantage of the horse's natural musculature and abilities. As my trainer taught it to me, the method's foundation is the walk. I spent untold hours schooling my mentor's horses (and not a few of my own) by walking alongside them, often loose in the round ring but also often on a lead in the arena, gently tapping their bellies with the butt end of a whip, to gradually coax the horses to take longer strides forward with their back legs. The horse's natural walk has the rear hoof step forward in exactly the track where the horse's fore hoof landed, rear stride precisely in fore stride. Yet by extending the rear stride farther forward than the fore hoof landed, rear stepping past the fore hoof's mark at first an inch or two but, with diligent ground training, six, eight, twelve, or more inches, the horse draws its rear quarter farther under its forequarter. A horse's ability to lift itself up in high gait, spin on a dime, and dance athletically in all gaits around the ring depends on precisely that drawing of the hindquarter under the forequarter. Nothing gets done without the horse's hindquarter lifting up the horse's forequarter. Hence, the proper, long-striding walk as foundation.

Foundations then need structure atop them. The two-track is a next step that my mentor trainer and other classical riders would use to further draw the horse's hindquarters under, elevating the forequarters and giving the horse its natural, high-stepping athleticism. A two-track involves requiring the horse to walk, trot, and canter somewhat sideways, initially by moving its head outward toward the rail in a shoulder-out maneuver, easier to begin, and then gradually to a shoulder-in maneuver along the rail, and finally to a correct two-track diagonally across the rectangular ring with the horse remaining parallel to the ring's long side. These maneuvers not only require the horse to draw the hind legs further under than simple straight tracking but also teach the horse to respond to a pressure of one of the rider's legs, the horse's side moving away from that pressure. Gradually, the horse learns to draw both hind legs under when the rider supplies the rider's two-leg pressure to both the horse's sides. The horse at first responds to the rider's heel or calf in the horse's ribs but gradually to merely subtle tensions of the rider's lower legs or even upper legs, until the rider controls the left, right, and forward actions of the horse nearly from the rider's own seat, with any movements of the rider's legs barely evident. Slight shifts and tensions of the rider's buttocks cue the horse to move left, right, and forward with increasing amounts of weight shifted from the horse's front to its rear quarters.

The rider must simultaneously maintain proper control of the horse's headset and neck and head movements using the reins and bit. To many trainers, the mechanical action of the bit seems critical to controlling the horse's headset, meaning the higher arch of its neck with its chin drawn in to make the forehead roughly perpendicular to the ground. Trainers will use every kind of bit from the simple snaffle to double bridles with snaffle and curb, all the way to high-spade bits with large tongue rollers and chain curb straps. The various bits supply more force or less force downward on the bars of the horse's mouth (a gap between the front teeth and rear molars) and upward against the horse's mouth roof. Yet to the classical trainer like my horse-whisperer mentor, the type of bit is less important than the means of its use. Above all, the trainer's hand on the reins must be firm, relaxed, and steady, so that the horse's mouth also remains relaxed and steady while the horse's head and neck move in balanced and rhythmic action around the steady bit. The rein must pass up from the bottom of the rider's relaxed hand and out between the thumb and forefinger so that the horse's pull on the rein naturally pinches the rein between thumb and forefinger, leaving the rest of the fingers including the pinky finger to gently guide the rein action.

When a classical trainer has a horse fully strengthened, balanced, and in hand, the trainer can stimulate the horse to the greatest natural degree and yet direct its enormous flight-instinctual energy inward and upward more so than outward and forward. The effect, greatest at an animated, park-style trot, is that the horse literally floats a foot or even two feet above the ground as each hoof digs deep into the ground, shooting the horse and its rider in bounding strides more upward than forward. To make the most-animated entry into a show ring, sale ring, or other exhibition with his most-talented park horse, my mentor trainer would encourage the grooms to shake bleach bottles with rocks, pop whips with plastic bags tied to the ends of their lashes, and otherwise raise such ruckus as to utterly energize the horse, which yet because of its exquisite training would not dash off in full flight but instead swell and rise up, ever higher, until it was flinging its forelegs out parallel to the ground and bounding deeper and higher off its hind legs without gaining any speed, instead just carrying ever higher its perfectly poised and tuxedo-appointed rider. The effect stunned the observer who had previously not imagined the possibility of such poised and yet furious athleticism. Behold, the horse, conqueror of continents and carrier of kings, greatest of all earthly creatures save his human master.

I only rarely and briefly could achieve anything approximating what my mentor trainer regularly achieved in this fashion with assorted mounts. The crazy horse Bert that my wife discovered, with me as his rider, could maintain that superb high park trot for good stretches at a time, but in that case the achievement was Bert's natural talent and my long strengthening of him, not my mastery of classical equitation. Trainers need not have great physical strength, although training does take physical stamina, balance, and timing. Training itself, though, is more a matter of illusion, of convincing the horse that performing beyond its own perceived capabilities is not just possible but the best idea. I once told my trainer that I wished that I was as strong as he was so that I could gather the horse in my rein hands the way that he did. He just laughed, saying that I was plenty strong enough, probably stronger than he was, but that it wasn't a matter of strength. To prove it, he would get on one of my horses, say Elixir, and promptly elevate his trotting action from a superior English horse, which was the most that I could make of him, into the caliber of a winning park horse. My mentor did the same with a difficult park horse Czestan that I tried hard to bring to winning form but never quite fully managed. If I could have wrung one final skill from my years of hard training work, much of it fitting and strengthening my mentor's best horses, then it would have been to be able to so elevate a superior English horse into a fine park horse. Riding a park horse feels like conquering worlds, not only when one enters a competition or exhibition ring to the gasps of the crowd but even when training alone on a dusty dirt road. One feels then that one can glorify God in all such contingencies.

5

Tack

    The first item of any consequence that I ever bought was not a car, guitar, or gaming console but a Shirley Brown western saddle. A new saddle is expensive, something for which a teenager must long save. Buying the Shirley Brown took most of what I had saved out of my youthful earnings. Shirley, in case you are wondering, was a horseman, not a horsewoman, a designer of the most comfortable, functional, working Western saddle that one could find. My mentor trainer had seen the amateur equipment that I was using and gradually helped me replace it with professional gear. The Shirley Brown was his first significant recommendation, a purchase that I never regretted. Over the ensuing years, I literally wore out the new saddle until it had no remaining salvage value, despite that a Western saddle is not generally the saddle of choice for training Arabian horses. Although Arabs do show Western, their greater performance achievement and value is in English or park. Most trainers thus train in an English flat saddle of the type that those fancier performance categories require. They wouldn't be caught dead riding their English and park horses in a Western saddle. The Shirley Brown, though, was different. It had the flat profile of an English flat saddle, with a low cantle and saddle horn, but its Western bulk and horn gave a rider a security that flat saddles cannot offer. You could really knock around on a horse, like run it into and out of a corner repeatedly for strengthening, agility, response, and submissiveness, without losing your seat. Using the Shirley Brown gave the rider an upper hand in every perilous riding situation, which is what a saddle should do.

I know because I had a few of those perilous situations. My mentor trainer's son was a practical jokester. His father had for a song bought a bunch of half-wild horses from a poor farmer down South as a favor. They took the farm's nine-horse trailer down, picked up the nutty horses, and on return dumped them into run-down stalls and paddocks around an old barn across the dirt road from the owner's fancy stable. Whenever things got a little slow, which wasn't often, the trainer would send one of us over to the old barn to get one of the half-wild horses to break and train, so my mentor could sell it. Well, my mentor trainer had sent his oldest son across the road to bring back and break to ride a tall, muscled, golden-colored three-year-old stallion, then just about the nuttiest of the bunch. The stallion was a handful just to halter and lead, no less think of riding. My mistake was to believe the son when he told me a couple days later that he had already broken the stallion to ride, if I wouldn't mind just hopping on it for a little more workout. Foolishly taking the bait, I just barely managed to saddle and mount the still-wild stallion, unknown to me *for his first time* and thus not in the cautious and humane way that we ordinarily broke green horses. To the great delight of my mentor's son, I have never had such a wild ride as that stallion gave me as he rushed headlong from one end of the arena to the other, crashing into the walls at each end. I just barely managed to stay on only because of my trusty Shirley Brown saddle.

By contrast, a flat saddle is a poor source of security. I hardly fell off horses at all, despite some earnest efforts by various horses. A couple years of riding bareback up and down the dirt roads around my parents' farm had helped me gain a pretty secure seat and balance. One time that I did fall off, which my wife remembers quite well, I could blame the stupid flat saddle. I was riding an older dark-liver-colored stallion imported from Poland where he had raced, which was precisely my problem. We were at a show that used a cordoned-off part of a racetrack in front of its grandstand for the show ring. Back at my home training stable, this stallion had been a darling horse, talented and fiery but entirely sweet and manageable. I relished showing him for my new horse-training client, a generous and well-respected breeder of other talented horses. Yet on the racetrack where I was about to show him, the stallion felt at any moment like he was prepared to take full flight, never mind the intentions of his rider. He also suddenly exhibited the strange habit of whirling around just before bolting, which is the way his races in

Poland had started, not by starting gate but in turn-and-bolt fashion. Warming the stallion up for a park class, I had on my nicest but also slipperiest riding suit, perched precariously atop the equally insecure flat saddle. One too many whirls, and the stallion had me clinging to the side of the saddle as he continued his pirouettes, knowing that I was a goner. Fortunately, he only ran back to our stall area in the barns, where my grooms promptly caught him. I caught up with the stallion a few moments later, dusty, none the worse for wear, but disgusted with myself, a disgust made worse by the great humor with which my wife took the occasion. I don't think that I'd fallen off a horse at a horse show before. Flat saddles and slippery suits make a difference.

Riding chaps are one of the comforts and conceits that many trainers use to save their scuffed legs and blistered knees, and stick better to the saddle, when training. Chaps, of course, are a Western adaptation, but trainers of English, park, jumping, dressage, and other performance horses will often wear chaps when training, saving the fancier but less-comfortable and less-sticky attire for the show ring. Chaps also look cool, or at least my wife has told me that she thought so, attributing our marriage in part to my having worn them around her. I wore chaps to ride whenever I could, so much so that when I took off my regular set of chaps, they would stand up all on their own due to their hard wearing, soaked and dried in salty human and horse sweat. Their poor condition didn't matter. I was putting them right back on for the next horse. Riding in jeans or other pants felt like exposing one's bony knees to razors, leaving as it did cherry-red contusions that took days to heal. Wrapping one's knees in bandages when riding was sometimes a necessity and other times an alternative to chaps but also an annoyance and incomplete palliative.

Shopping for chaps, Western bridles, Western hats, and other Western wear and gear was a hoot. In the days before online ordering, getting the best price and selection meant stopping at one or more of the premier Western-wear outlets in Oklahoma City when passing through on other horse business. The places were spectacular, with the glitter of abundant silver, row upon row of hats, boots, and saddles, and smelling of leather. I once bought a new pair of Western-style work boots on the way to the National Championships in Albuquerque. Believe it or not, walking-style Western boots can be extremely comfortable in which to work when you must be on your feet or on horseback all day. We got to Albuquerque a couple of weeks early to help the horses adjust to the altitude, for last-minute show preparation, and frankly for fun. On an off day, my mentor sent us up the tram to the top of Sandia Peak outside Albuquerque. His oldest son, the jokester, decided at the last minute to walk down the mountain rather than ride the tram back down. He had the car keys, so I felt little choice but to follow him. What could go wrong? Four hours and a dodged rattlesnake later, we limped into the dark parking lot and headed back to the ranch where we had boarded the horses. Thank God for my comfortable new Western boots, although after a long walk down a mountain, they no longer looked so new.

While the fancy bridles, bits, and saddles get most of the attention when one thinks of horse tack, my mentor knew some helpful things about the working tack that makes the bigger difference in training. One of the first things that I learned had to do with the lead-line chain and lunging chain that handlers routinely use to help control rambunctious horses. Most handlers would run a short chain through the halter ring and over the bridge of the horse's nose, clipping the chain to the ring on the halter's other side. A pull on the lead or lunge line pulls the chain down on the bridge of the horse's nose, a decent control point. The problem with that configuration, though, is that when one pulls on the lead or lunge, the chain tends to catch, cinch, and lock down over the nose's bridge even when the handler releases the tension. That locking action destroys the corrective effect of a brief tug on the lead or lunge, drawing it out into a punitive pain relieved only by a sharp toss of the horse's head. You can ruin a horse simply by using this too-short chain. The solution is to run a longer chain all the way around the nose, clipping the chain back to itself so that it remains a free loop. A tug on the lead or line pulls the chain down across the bridge of the nose only as briefly as the tug itself, the release of which also instantly releases the chain. One thus gets the proper corrective effect without the punitive pain and following toss of the horse's head.

My mentor trainer shared another, similar piece of equipment, one that he called a *figure eight*, used for similar purposes. The figure eight was just a twenty or thirty-foot length of narrow acrylic rope with which one could lead and lunge an especially difficult horse, instead of the standard lunge rope clipped to the halter or with the nose-looped chain.

The trick was to make a sliding figure-eight shape out of the rope's end, around the horse's nose and up over the poll at the top of the horse's head. A tug on the rope would thus constrict the rope around the nose but also pull down on the sensitive poll, with the pressure at both nose and poll released the instant that the tug released. Once again, used properly, a figure eight can supply just enough corrective effect without any lasting irritant or punitive pain. The horse feels quite free until the trainer tugs lightly on the figure eight but then feels quite free instantly again on tug's release, which is the action that a sensitive trainer needs to condition the horse's response. I used the figure eight to good effect and many times saw my mentor also do so, especially at exhibitions where the host would induce my mentor to humanely quell and control a notoriously wild horse, to the crowd's amazement. We often used the figure eight for the exhibition of loading the horse in a trailer.

The most-powerful piece of training equipment my mentor used, though, was the aforesaid running W, appropriate only for horses that demonstrated no respect for the superior intelligence and authority of their masters. Training's purpose is not to break the horse's spirit. To the contrary, to induce superior performance, trainers need a horse's greatest energies. Breaking the horse's spirit in a way that causes it to lose its instinctual sensitivity including its flight response, that which gives it such life and animation, and causing the horse to refuse to offer its full frame and musculature pursing the trainer's ends, would be to eliminate that which attracts us to horses. Instead, the breaking that trainers sometimes find necessary is to reduce or eliminate a horse's desire to overcome and even to harm the trainer. Horses have several ways that they can seriously injure their handlers or destroy tack, equipment, and property, including kicking, cow-kicking (a forward kick rather than rearward kick with the hindfoot), striking, biting, stepping and stomping with their hooves, and bulling and pinning using their large frame and great weight. The running W is a humane way of showing a horse that it has no present need to defend itself from or attack, dominate, and hurt, a trainer. The running W is a thin acrylic rope traveling from the trainer's hand through a tiny pulley on the near side of the surcingle, down to a pulley on a soft cuff around one fore ankle, up to another pulley in the middle of the girth, down to a cuff on the other fore ankle, and up to the surcingle's far side. Pulling on the rope as the horse moves forward draws the horse's forelegs under it so that it must kneel no matter how hard it wishes to run, kick, strike, or fight.

I say that the method is humane, and it is when properly employed. The point is not the trainer's dominance as much as the horse's peaceful submission, relaxation, and even comfort. Horses that bite, strike, and kick at their trainers and handlers suffer a destructive anger and tension. One too many such acts, and the horse is off to the slaughterhouse, judged too dangerous for human handling. Even if the mean horse's owner judges it too valuable to destroy, the horse faces a difficult life made so miserable only by its own resentment-fueled danger. One short session with the running W can reduce or eliminate that resentment, in a process that an old-time trainer would call *sacking out* the horse. Once the horse kneels due to the restraint of the running W, the trainer can gently induce it to lay the rest of the way down, a safe, submissive, and naturally relaxing position for any horse. The trainer can then stroke and massage the horse without the horse exhibiting the tension that its mean streak would cause it to exhibit if standing. The trainer can even take a soft saddle blanket or grain sack with which to rub and then gently thump the horse (the sacking-out part) until the horse accepts the gentle treatment with the reassurance that it warrants—in other words, without kicking, which a horse cannot do while laying down, or even any tension or flinching. The process is, in short, demonstrative, certain, and reassuring. When the trainer permits the formerly mean but now thoroughly gentled horse to rise again after a couple of minutes, the horse will shake itself off and smack its lips in a relaxed and satisfied gesture, like it has just left behind its former miserable life for a new life of trust and confidence in its trainer, and peaceful and productive effort. Without the running W, man-killing, buggy-destroying terrors would remain so, but with it, they join the parade of productive horses in procession to their natural end.

Running Ws and figure eights, though, are merely rarely used special tools. By contrast, the surcingle, a padded leather strap encircling the horse's midsection, is an everyday training staple, the trainer's best friend. The surcingle enables a trainer to accustom a young horse to a girth passing under the ticklish belly, a constraining irritant to which some young horses at first object. The surcingle also accustoms the horse to side reins hooked from the surcingle to the bit and driving lines passing through rings on the surcingle's side, both for fitting the horse and as a prelude to riding or driving. Introducing a young horse to the surcingle usually doesn't take much but on occasion presents challenges. I once had a talented-looking two-year-old colt whose owner wanted me to show the colt at halter in the coming summer. To fit the colt, I started the colt lunging in circles around me on a thirty-foot lunge line and then had him walk and trot over cavalletti (miniature wooden jumps) for balance and strengthening. The colt and I were soon bored with the work, and so I hoped next to flex and strengthen the colt's neck, and sweat and trim its throatlatch, with bridle, bit, and surcingle, before introducing driving lines. We never quite got past the surcingle. The moment that I snugged its girth lightly around his midsection as we walked side by side, the surcingle's constriction under his sensitive belly caused him to explode in stiff-legged, frog-like leaps. The funny thing, though, was that with each landing, he would emit a loud, strange bray, catapulting him into the next leap. I was less alarmed than embarrassed for him. My wife turned my embarrassment acute, though, when she came running out of the end of the barn toward the outdoor paddock in which I was working the colt. I thought that she had come running out of concern for my safety or the security of the poor colt, but instead she was looking up and pointing toward the sky proclaiming excitedly, *The geese are coming! The geese are coming!* No, the geese were not yet returning from the South. My frog-leaping colt just sounded like one. We cannot to this day recall the event without a good laugh.

 Other training tack isn't so functional as the Shirley Brown saddle or the simple surcingle, instead more ornamental. Showing an Arab in a Western class meant having a saddle with sterling silver, generally the more silver the better. Some saddles had so much silver on them that one could hardly see the underlying leather. Trainers would also show in Western classes with silver-encrusted breast pieces, bridles, and reins. Rules required the saddles to have lariats and hobbles tied to them for certain Western classes, a provision for which tack shops must have lobbied because no one would ever put an Arab horse in hobbles, and few if any Arabs make good roping horses. The biggest sterling-silver conceit, though, was the silver spade bits. Silversmiths would overlay the bit's elaborate, S-shaped shanks with sterling silver etched with elaborately detailed patterns. The bits looked gorgeous on a good Western horse, although not all horses could tolerate the large spades typical of their design. The spade is the prominent part of the bit's bar that rests on the horse's tongue. A tug on the reins levers the spade up toward the roof of the horse's mouth, an inducement for the horse to tuck its chin in the elegant manner that judges reward. I trained and showed one stallion that, as beautiful as he looked and as well as he performed in my silver spade bit, could not tolerate the spade, suddenly flipping himself over backward out of fright at it even without a tug on the reins. When he did so to our complete shock as we tacked him up at a show, he landed on and crushed one of our tack trunks, which as it collapsed let out from its inside a big puff of white baby powder, used to make horse's socks whiter. Once we confirmed that the stallion was alright, my wife and the grooms laughed hysterically over the spectacle of the big puff of white powder. I didn't think it so funny because I still had to ride the back-flipping horse.

Trainers take strong interest in their tack, to the point of both designing tack and, in some cases, making it. My mentor designed ingenious sliding reins, elastic side reins, bits, horseshoes, and other equipment, devices, and contraptions that he would ask leather shops, blacksmiths, and other craftsmen to produce. Admirably, a former apprentice of my mentor somehow made his own silver spade bits, so sensitively balanced and ornately adorned as to make them much in demand. I could not imagine the skill that such fine silversmithing would take, but I did do some leather work, frequently repairing my own surcingle and other tack, and making my own working bridle and reins. Leather work satisfies the craftsman's urge while also serving the necessities of training, thus making a great evening pastime for a bone-weary trainer. Cleaning tack is another satisfyingly simple yet essential pursuit, embellished by the smell of Murphy's oil soap in bar or bottle form, the squish of the sponge, and the dark leather's supple feel. Tack gets dirty quickly from horse lather, trainer sweat, and arena dust, the latter a horse trainer's bane. We were constantly watering arenas in fruitless efforts to keep down the choking dust, ground to the finest measure by constant pounding from the trained horse's hooves.

Two-wheel and four-wheel buggies were the most-expensive piece of training and showing equipment. Arabian horses show in more different performance classes than many other breeds. Those classes include not only the core park, English, and Western riding classes, plus sometimes stock, trail, dressage, and even jumping classes, but also pleasure driving with a two-wheel cart and formal driving with a four-wheel buggy. The carts with which a trainer breaks and trains a driving horse are rugged, usually with steel shafts that only bend rather than break if a difficult horse tests them. The show carts, though, have long, thin, wooden shafts, no match at all for any weight that an unruly horse may wish to throw against them. Snapping a wooden shaft first means quelling the horse that broke it and then shipping the broken buggy (if a two-wheeler) or the broken shaft piece (if a four-wheeler) off for expensive repair. Trust me, I know. I never had a horse break a show buggy, although I had more than one bend the training cart's metal shafts. One horse, a small three-year-old mare the owner of which sent to me specifically and solely to break to drive, rammed my indestructible training cart's shaft into the arena wall, knocking trophies off the wall in the observation room on the wall's other side. Miracle of miracles, a couple of weeks later, the owner safely drove the young mare several miles home without incident, from my standpoint, one of my better thirty-day wonders (as trainers call the short-term miracles that owners of lesser means often expect of their services). I did once break off the tips of both shafts of a two-wheel show cart, though, when I stupidly loaded it upright on the back of a six-horse trailer that I then drove under a low overpass. Trainers aren't always smarter than their horses.

Aside from tack, trainers or their spouses, partners, or friends must also give substantial attention to the trainer's show dress. Each different class has its different dressing conventions. Park competitions require the most formal dress, one's best riding suit or even a riding-adapted tuxedo with top hat. Trainers go to special tailors for custom-fit riding suits, longer in the coat and tails than a business suit, and with longer trousers with a bell bottom to go over the riding boot, held in place with straps. The trousers have extra material sewn over the inside of the knee where chafing would quickly wear through single-thickness material. My wife and I learned from another trainer of the Lexington tailor who fits Saddlebred riders with their best riding suits. We visited the famous Lexington Junior League Horse Show at Lexington's Red Mile racetrack and, while in Lexington, ordered and got fitted for suits at the tailor, while also picking up smart-looking English bowler hats. The dress for Western classes is of course completely different, right down to the fancy chaps and cowboy hat.

While visiting fancy Western tack shops or a fancy tailor of formal suits near Lexington's Red Mile may sound like fun, and it was, the greater fun that my wife and I shared was visiting an ancient tack shop located incongruously in a poor downtown neighborhood in a nearby Midwestern city. A tack shop has little business being in a busy metropolitan city, but this shop was so old that it may have been there when horses still pulled wagons and buggies along the city's streets. Indeed, the charm of it was partly in the good likelihood of discovering a great old saddle for a very decent price somewhere deep in a stack of saddles within one of its many tiny, dark rooms or in its dusty basement. The place also smelled of fine old leather, one of the best smells around. Another charm of the place was the two old men who ran it. In candor, they were not in the least charming, rather grumpy and gruff, although my wife could warm them up, just as she can warm up most grumbling service providers. Yet the two old men knew their trade, not only repairing saddles but also making them. And although they hardly looked like horsemen, they seemed to know from a design standpoint the strengths and weaknesses of each model and brand. We were always in a hurry to get back to the farm, but I wished sometimes that I could have fallen into a deep dream in the place, like Rip Van Winkle. Maybe, after all, horse world was just a dream from an old tack shop.

6

Trainers

Horse trainers depend for their living on their ability to impress horse owners that they can add value to their horses greater than the cost of training. The calculus is easier for private trainers who work for a single owner managing the owner's farm. The farm needs management that the private trainer provides, independent of the value that the trainer adds or fails to add to any of the owner's individual horses. A private trainer will feed, breed, foal, pasture, transport, buy, sell, and otherwise care for the owner's horses, while also maintaining the farm by mowing fields, painting fences, and even cleaning stalls, before thinking of training the farm's better horses. That management and simple labor keeps the private trainer employed even when the training doesn't go so well, perhaps failing to produce any show winners leading to breeding fees and horse sales. Some owners are quite capable of funding, and quite happy to fund, a losing farm out of other income, whether family wealth or business earnings. The private trainer is simply part of the cost while also often a large part of the fellowship, pleasure, and joy. Private trainers can make great companions to and foils for prominent owners of private stables. My wife and I managed a private farm for a time for a wealthy owner whose family we got to know and enjoy.

The more-interesting specimens, though, are the public trainers, interesting because they wholly depend on the confidence of their individual horse-training clients, a confidence that they must continually engender with their show wins and other fruits of their training skills. A public trainer has no rich benefactor employing the trainer simply to manage the stable. Rather, the public trainer may have a dozen or more clients, some rich but others middle income and some even relatively poor, whom the trainer must continually satisfy warrant the monthly training fees due for their horses. The clients typically own a smaller farm that does not warrant a full-time trainer or may even own no farm at all but only a horse or two that they deem worthy of training. I was for several years a public trainer, with the devoted support of my hard-working, horse-loving young wife. We trained horses owned by doctors, dentists, lawyers, police chiefs, schoolteachers, construction contractors, service providers, and small-business owners, among others.

Horse trainers can be colorful. Some trainers need the color, to gain public attention, win clients, and then entertain clients even when their horses are not so successful. A trainer may be skilled and hard-working but have clients whose horses have only modest talents. A trainer's business income grows and shrinks with the quality of the clients' horses. One winning horse can attract clients to send their own steeds to the trainer in the hope that the trainer can work similar wonders. A trainer who hits a dry spell of inadequate horse talent will scuffle until another winner appears, attracting the ambitions of other clients who once again supply the necessary stock to keep the public trainer floating. Public trainers facing an especially difficult time, such as in the off season when owners have less urgency to send a horse, may have to take other work, things like manufacturing work, farming, bookkeeping, or whatever their other skills permit, to carry them over. Penurious clients need thirty-day, sixty-day, and ninety-day miracles out of their trainers, while trainers know that doing a thorough job of training a good horse can take six months, nine months, a year, or more.

My wife and I had one indigent client, a schoolteacher with a passel of growing children, who owned a white stallion just handsome enough to win some local classes and gain some breeding fees. Dreaming of riches, the client hired us to show the stallion at a National Championship but insisted that the client's son groom the horse to save on training and show fees. Unfortunately, the son clipped the horse's grey muzzle with the wrong clipper blades, so tight that the horse's formerly white muzzle showed only the black skin. The effect was to make the poor horse look like it had dipped its beautiful white head halfway up in a bucket of black paint. I was so disgusted and embarrassed that I almost refused to show the horse. After all, at a National Championship, *my* reputation was at stake just as much as the *stallion's* reputation. After serious reflection, I decided to take the hit and show the now-hopeless contender anyway, despite the perfectly obvious embarrassment. And sure enough, one of the three judges made a big show of inspecting closely, and even wiping with his hand, the stallion's super-black snout to see if we had illegally colored it. As the judge did so, I half-whispered something to him about the groom's stupid mistake, over which the judge had a good quiet laugh that I am sure he shared with the other judges when the class was over.

When I was training, the nation's leading trainer was the mature, urbane, and very talented son of a wealthy physician who had imported from Poland the Arabian breed's most spectacularly talented and successful sire Bask. Bask, himself a National Champion, sired countless other National Champions, many of them trained and shown by this one trainer. Not in any way to diminish his considerable talent, the trainer had the perfect mix of exquisite horses with incredible performance capability, wealthy clients clamoring to have him show those horses, and the most-elaborate facilities and best staffs to support the training work. The trainer had also closely studied the mechanical, fitting, and grooming methods of the nation's best Saddlebred trainers, adapting them for use with Arabian horses. The combination was unstoppable, enabling his father, brother, and family to build a small empire funded by spectacular auctions at which celebrities appeared to buy horses. Celebrities were not unusual in the Arabian breed. The longtime Las Vegas entertainer Wayne Newton was an early breeder, as was the Broadway playwright Mike Nichols. I once shook the hand of Arabian owner, pop singer, and television host John Davidson at a National Championship (he pulled my name out of a hat at the competition's celebratory drawing—seriously) and also met horse-investor and basketball star Kareem Abdul-Jabbar and Billy Graham's daughter Anne Graham Lotz at another big event.

The horse-whisperer trainer under whom I apprenticed, at the time managing a large private farm owned by an automotive-industry magnate, was a completely different and rare breed among horse trainers. My mentor grew up a Virginia farm boy who swam with the Chincoteague ponies. He had worked every kind of horse in his rural childhood and youth, and yet had later traveled to the Spanish Riding School in Vienna to study its famed Lipizzaner stallions and known the greatest circus trainer of all time. My mentor wasn't just a fine trainer of Arabian show horses. He could train horses to do *anything* of which a horse of any breed was physically capable. My mentor had more training talent in his little finger than I would hope to accumulate in a lifetime.

My mentor burnished his high standing with me by once telling me a story about the world's greatest circus trainer whom my mentor had seen and met, and whose methods he had pursued. Horse acts were once a big part of circuses, when traveling circuses were once a big part of culture and entertainment. I could imagine my mentor, the Virginia farm boy whose father and grandfather had worked their farm with horses, traveling some distance with his family to see the circus while wanting especially to see the horse acts. The famous circus trainer's act, executed on a resplendent white horse, did not disappoint. The famous trainer, dressed in the most-formal riding wear including top hat, had his resplendent steed perform all the high maneuvers of the Haute Ecole, even the most-difficult leap into the air with the violent rear kick out. The famous trainer had then ridden his exquisite horse out of the ring at the artificially high-stepping Spanish trot. The crowd roared for an encore, but what more could rider and horse do? Yet in came the famous trainer mounted on the white steed, still performing the spectacular Spanish trot... but now doing it *backward*. No other horse was ever known to be so strong, balanced, submissive, smart, and gloriously in hand as to accomplish the feat, which might be somewhat akin to an equine Michael Jackson doing a leaps and bounds moonwalk.

While my mentor shared other stories often, this story I heard only once and not with others present. He told it just for me, I believe I figured rightly, because I had served him well and loyally. Indeed, my mentor's success relied in part on earnest apprentices, one at a time, who would give everything to learn from the master. As exhilarating as it can be, horse training is always also exhausting mentally, physically, and spiritually. My mentor could not sustain it alone, even though he was still in his forties when I worked under him. I didn't know it when I began apprenticing for him, but he had other apprentices before me, and he would have others to follow. I discovered what should have been obvious when I met one of his former apprentices at a distant, cross-country show to which my mentor had taken me both to groom and, unusually, to show-ride some of his horses. Usually, only my mentor rode his horses at the shows, or maybe one of his sons would ride one, never an apprentice and certainly not a groom. But at this one show, I rode, winning an important preliminary class toward competing for the show's performance championship. But my mentor inexplicably did not ask me to ride again in the championship class. We just left unfinished that bit of business that we had so well started.

While I wasn't disappointed at the lost opportunity to finish what I had started, by riding again and maybe winning the championship for which I had qualified his mount, and I certainly didn't hold the lost opportunity against my mentor, the show ended up a turning point. That turning started when at the show I met my trainer's former apprentice. I knew of him as a fine, still-young trainer, and I knew that he knew my mentor, but until he introduced himself to me, I hadn't known that he had once done the years of grunt work that I was doing for my mentor. After some friendly talk about the sort of things that horse trainers find interesting, meaning horses, tack, bits, training techniques, and other trainers, he confided in me not only that he had been my mentor's apprentice and that he owed his own skill and success to that apprenticeship but also that when he had eventually returned home to his own training work, my mentor had abruptly ended their friendship. He kindly offered me his counsel, support, and friendship if I had a similarly difficult experience. The conversation, still among relative strangers, was among the most bittersweet I have ever had.

The influence of a mentor trainer with whom one lives, works, and travels is profound and unavoidable. Indeed, influence is exactly what an apprentice seeks. Yet young apprentices to master horse trainers soon find themselves not just training like their mentor but also dressing, walking, and talking like the mentor, right down to the same expressions, demeanor, and accent. For me, the phenomenon was disturbing. I didn't want to lose who I was, just wanted instead to become a better horse trainer, but the subconscious pull feels irresistible. Fortunately, my mentor had few if any bad habits, none at least that I could readily discern. He certainly didn't smoke, drink, or chase women, and, unusual for horsemen, didn't even swear. He was, though, a country boy from

Virginia with a heavy accent and distinct carriage and demeanor, distinct from my own Midwestern roots, and yet I was soon walking and talking like him.

Quite naturally, because of maturation and job responsibilities, I had to leave my mentor's employ not long after that distant show with him where I met his former apprentice. While we didn't remain close, he nonetheless treated me decently, apparently unlike he had treated the former apprentice. Still, on one occasion I did unwittingly and unwillingly experience the uncomfortable role around him of *former* apprentice. The summer after I left my mentor's employ, I had great success showing at halter an expensive and heralded young stallion Sayyid that seemed destined for breeding. The stallion didn't lose all summer. But with the all-important year-end Futurity competition coming up, his owners invited my mentor to critique my showmanship of Sayyid to better prepare for the Futurity. Now, I hadn't shown Sayyid that summer using any of my mentor's techniques but instead some emerging, still largely secret techniques that other trainers had developed about which I had learned through observation, grooms, and the trainer grapevine. My mentor's gifts were in fitting and training horses for anything other than halter competition, even though he had shown a halter National Champion. I knew this fact, as did every other trainer but unfortunately not Sayyid's owners. And sure enough, my mentor's critique went badly. I was doing everything all wrong, he said with a look of disgust mixed with disappointment that I still remember after having hoped, foolishly, instead to impress him. He swiftly corrected me in front of the owners. Abandoning the new method that I had discovered and employed to win throughout the summer, and instead using my mentor's modest technique, I lost the Futurity to a horse that we'd beaten all summer.

Although they are competitors against one another, horse trainers tend to treat one another exceedingly well. The work is just too hard, dangerous, and uncertain to treat poorly others who pursue it with you. For example, when a driving horse kicked and broke the jaw of one trainer, requiring some time off while his wired-shut jaw healed, other trainers generously helped out with his show string. For me, a big benefit of showing was the informal, outside-the-ring interaction with other trainers. Except for the shows, training is isolating. You work alone with the horse, at your own stable. You work one horse for a half-hour to an hour before handing it off to a groom who hands you the next horse for another half-hour to hour, one horse after another all day. You may chat with the groom for a couple of minutes in the handoffs, but you have no one with whom to speak when working the horses. The work is not like a dentist's office where the professionals chat all day long with the patients. Horses don't talk. At shows, though, trainers work their horses around other trainers, often in crowded rings where a trainer can walk a horse alongside another trainer's horse to chat with the other trainer or stand at ringside chatting with another trainer while waiting for the groom to bring out another horse to work. Some trainers keep to themselves, but most find friendships with other trainers in which they can share the joys and challenges of the work.

When my wife and I left my parents' farm to become public trainers at a well-appointed dressage stable, we needed that collegial mentoring of other trainers. We loved our life together on the farm, training horse after horse. We rented a wing of the stable in which we kept our clients' Arabian horses, sharing the indoor ring, outdoor rings, and paddocks with horses of other breeds belonging to the stable's owner and his adult children, including another public trainer but in the different dressage pursuit. In many ways, that time was idyllic. My wife and I would exhaust ourselves each day doing our best to make something of the motley crew of horses our modest clientele had entrusted to us. The shows, though, supplied the community, information, and education that we needed. One training couple was incredibly kind to take us under their wing. They were older by about ten or fifteen years, with two pre-teen children. Their well-connected clients had supplied them with good horses, generally though not uniformly better than our own. They were winning a lot, while we were winning only a little. They must easily have seen how innocent we were of what public training truly required, and so they politely insisted that we join them for a meal now and then at the horse-show cafeteria, and later invited us to their farm on a couple of occasions. My wife and I treasured their friendship and learned from them a great deal of the practical side of maintaining a public training stable. May God bless them richly for their kindness.

My mentor trainer and his wife had another trainer couple who were their good friends, although their friends trained for a private farm on the other side of the country, and so as far as I could tell, they saw one another only at the annual National Championships. One could easily see the affinity around which they formed and maintained their friendship. Both couples were country folk, salt-of-the-earth types, proud descendants from a bygone horse-and-stock era, not at all cosmopolitan and sophisticated like many of the premier trainers were or pretended to be as they tried to attract sophisticated, rich, professional and entertainer clients. The other trainer, my mentor's best friend, would tell his apprentices and grooms to be sure to get a good education because training was no guarantee of a job, and you should always have something to fall back on. Other trainers and their wannabes would sneer when they heard of the advice, drawing their confidence from the Arabian breed right then being awash in money. I, though, tried to resist joining in the sneer, instead long remembering the other trainer's sage advice, notwithstanding the allure of the money, excitement, and celebrity washing over the breed.

Trainers do each have their own identity, which goes a long way to attract clients and hold their confidence and interest. One trainer from the East Coast was a demanding perfectionist about everything including not only how his horses performed and looked but also his own clothing, the training stable's appointments and care (the barn's hallway constantly swept and watered-down with sweet-smelling antiseptic), his tack, everything. His style was also Broadway formal, spotlights shining on high-gloss black surfaces with red pinstriping, black patent-leather tack, formal suit, and bowler hat. Unfortunately, he was so demanding that at the end of one long show season his overworked grooms went to the Department of Labor for overtime wages that were so substantial that they bankrupted his public training stable. He came back the next year working for a single wealthy owner. Another trainer, though, would have a down-home or can-do style, entertaining hard-scrabble clients who had little to fund their training needs. Another trainer would be a playboy, smoking cigarettes and flirting with his female clients or wives of male clients. One trainer would be cheap, another extravagantly expensive. One would coddle horses, another would drive and dominate them. Owners had a good trainer array from which to choose.

The trainer with the most distinct style, though, was an older and frankly portly woman who, by appearances, might have been the least likely horse-trainer candidate. She was, though, outstanding, one of the very best trainers, sure to show nothing but winners, seldom stooping to anything less. Her style was Mary Poppins magic schoolmarm, tight hair bun, prim and proper in dress even when working about the barn, speaking very little but demanding very much of herself, her horses, and her grooms, and consistently producing magic performances. She didn't bother with Western classes, which were clearly beneath her. She showed a little at halter but was the absolute queen of the ring in park, English, driving, and combination classes. With her round frame and short little legs and arms tucked into a long-tailed riding coat, and her white gloves and black top hat, she would perch high atop an exquisite performance horse, holding her riding whip in a distinctive pointing-up style. She would then reach over with the little whip to give her spectacular mount a sharp tap, like a schoolmarm rapping the knuckles of a student whose writing had taken a sloppy turn, and off her horse would go giving its absolute best possible performance to try to meet her impossibly high standard. Because of her inflexibly high standards, she tended to attract clients who had a single outstanding horse to send her, the best that they had ever bred. Indeed, her clients could not afford to send her anything less than their best, or anything more than one horse at a time, because her services were clearly expensive. She owned and drove a rare Streamliner van, not a trailer but a *van*, appointed her show stalls with gorgeous red curtains, and somewhere hid a mousey husband whose sharp bookkeeping made it all work.

Whether for lack of insight or confidence, because of my younger age, or for other reason, I never quite developed or determined my own style. Maybe I had a style that I just could not discern. But I think instead that God had made me for a different world. Most trainers completely looked and acted the part, even if they each played the role somewhat or quite differently. They were lifers, and they knew it and loved it, growing larger in personality every year, drawing clients in their wake like groupies following a famous old band's unending road show. The show must go on, and it did because of their amusing, commanding, overcoming, eccentric, scurrilous, magical, or other identities and abilities. Me? I didn't know myself as anything other than an explorer passing through horse world while looking for a different promised land. I didn't know my destiny, but I knew it wasn't horse world, even though I celebrated, respected, and admired every trainer who in horse world had found their destiny. I just knew that I had to pass through for whatever the journey would teach me. As painful as some of the lessons were, horse world taught me a lot, every bit of which I treasure, especially to have attuned my soul beyond self to spirit.

7

Owners

Owners are a big part of the horse world equation, without which horse world largely wouldn't exist. Whatever their storied history as the beasts of war, transport, exploration, and burden, with which people discovered, won, built, and maintained empires and nations, horses are today a luxury, a collectible, no part of sustaining a modern economy and instead barely registering as a contributor, and for that only as diversion and recreation. No one needs a horse to get to work, plow the fields, or make a house call late at night to deliver a baby, or to win war's battles. Yes, the horse industry generates substantial commerce as a recreational pursuit or hobby, especially when the good times roll, but as a recreational, sporting, or leisure industry, horse world depends entirely on expendable income. In depression and recession, the bloom of the industry disappears, horse populations shrink, and their trainers find other jobs or go hungry.

Some hardened old lawyers share among themselves the sarcastic quip that law practice would be great but for the clients. Although I understand the source of the sentiment, residing in difficult clients facing awful consequences largely of their own making, I don't much like that quip because the law profession exists for clients, whom I routinely respected and always valued. I also respected and valued my horse-training clients, most of whom were patient, persevering, generous, caring, funny, and fun-loving, both in how they related to their horses and how they thought of and treated their horse trainers. As I recount briefly at the end of this book, the only employer to ever fire me was a horse owner, one whose farm my wife and I had managed until my wife left for other employment while I soldiered on to my ultimate termination. Yet I don't in the least hold the action against the owner. Rather, I continue to deeply appreciate the confidence that he showed me in entrusting his horses to me and in compensating me to, yes, work hard but also to work in a beautiful place with some special horses and to have some fun in the process. When all was said and done, he didn't owe me a day's more pay than he paid me and instead showed me considerable grace in the employment. At least, I say, don't bite the hand that feeds you.

One of our most-steadfast horse-training clients was the medical-administrator wife of a pediatric oncologist. Appreciate the burden of her husband's employment, trying to care for cancer-stricken children whom everyone knew were very likely to die at a very young age. Horse world was the wife's escape, where she could go to forget her husband's unremitting burden. She owned a fine young mare that had a personality much like her own—pert, perky, and irrepressible. The mare was just good enough at halter and under saddle to do just well enough to keep show competition fun and exciting, bringing home the occasional blue ribbon and many more ribbons of other colors. While her husband worked eighty-hour weeks trying to save the lives of children by, in effect, poisoning them with chemicals and radiation (as he once described to me his mostly futile efforts), she took time off from her more-regular medical-administrator work to travel to shows all over the region with friends, to meet more friends and to compete, win, lose, eat, laugh, and forget about dying children. Because she and her husband were both working professionals and had no farm of their own, we got to board her mare year round and train the mare much of that time. We thus were able to train and keep the mare fit for competition in English, Western, and driving, pursuits that absorbed the cheery owner's positive attention and abundant energies. She was the life of our show-to-show traveling owner party.

If that owner was the party's life, then other owners were the heart of our traveling road show. One very kind and patient business executive owned a young mare that she had us show at halter and then train and show under saddle, until owner and mare were ready to compete on their own together. Amateur owners, like the medical administrator and business executive, were a significant part of our training business. Their interest in developing their own riding and showing skill often made them longer-term clients. Training a horse is one thing. Training its owner is quite another thing, usually significantly longer term and more time-consuming. You think training a horse to do a horse's work is hard? Try training its schoolteacher, administrator, or business-person owner to do the work of a horse trainer. But over time, earnest owners who initially have little or no skill and even less aptitude can make solid and, in some cases, even good riders. This business executive became an accomplished amateur horsewoman, due more to her own perseverance than to the patient hours that we spent with her. A pharmaceutical-executive friend of hers, whose horse my mentor trained, had far less aptitude than she did but through years of hard knocks eventually won an amateur performance National Championship. He, too, was a horse-show regular and favorite, taking other owners and trainers out for meals at the shows and keeping everyone on good terms, despite stiff and increasingly high-stakes competition.

My wife and I enjoyed many other horse-training clients. We trained several horses for a kind and generous pet-store owner who was both an optimist about his horses and yet had a good eye for animal talent, perhaps from his pet-store business. His first horses, even a few that he had us show, weren't much, but he learned quickly. He soon acquired for a very reasonable price a filly that in a couple of years grew into a gorgeous mare, one that responded especially well to our halter training techniques. Some horses do only what they must, while others take the whole bait—hook, line and sinker. This mare, while still a good-looking animal with solid conformation when in the stall or out in the pasture, would transform herself into a champion when in the ring. She just seemed to stand on the tips of her hooves, growing two or three inches to take on the appearance of a complete diva in competition's excitement. Her pet-store owner was not, however, sentimental. Years of selling puppies and canaries, and of showing sales-training videos to his pet-store staff, had cured him of all sentiment even for a beautiful and quite-sweet young champion mare. He sold the mare for a handsome profit shortly after her biggest Regional Championships win. Fortunately, the pet-store owner was much more loyal to his trainer. He did a lot for us, even as we did a little for him.

Another unusually fun client owned an older light-chestnut stallion that we showed one summer at halter and Western. He owned a small manufacturing business that had produced sufficient excess revenue for him and his wife over the years that they had purchased and equipped a small, beautifully manicured gentleman's farm. They were a little later to horses, not long-time breeders but relatively new entrants and not overly ambitious about the pursuit but more appreciating the beauty of the animals and diversion and good health of the sport. The owner and his wife brought that good spirit to every show that they attended, which was only about half of the shows to which we took their handsome but not extraordinarily talented stallion. The owner, who respected our efforts whether we won or lost but was always overjoyed when we won, had such a warm personality that he kept everyone loose and laughing when he was around. My wife especially would giggle when the owner, an informal bear of a man, would rub his back up against a show tent post or scratch his back with a set of shears. That couple and a similarly good-natured couple owning a highway-repair business felt like the backbone of our small training business.

One other owner couple struck my wife and I as just plain decent folk, the salt of the American earth. Although they were a somewhat-older working couple without much disposable income, they nonetheless left a mare with us to break and train for a couple months for the wife to ride and enjoy back at their home. They visited as often as they could, every weekend at least and some weekday evenings, so that the wife could learn as much about training and riding and about her mare's preferences and peculiarities in the two late-summer months of training that they could afford. When we were done working their mare for them in the later afternoons, they would help us feed and water the horses, and sweep the barns. We would then sit out back of the barn chewing on a long stalk of grass and trying to cool down, while the husband would tell stories and share wisdom with us, a young couple in our early twenties who had a lot of wisdom to learn. They had quite a life up until then, giving the husband many good stories to tell, things like the husband, a trim and small man, having once weighed well over three-hundred pounds and spent years in prison. I don't remember anything specific of the husband's wisdom, just that it somehow served us well. Maybe the benefit was simply that the couple cared as much about us as their horse that we were training.

One evening listening to the husband's stories, the wife spotted a wild parakeet, surely one that had escaped from its owner's cage. The wife interrupted her husband to point out the parakeet flitting around, chasing seeds or insects a hundred feet away. *Catch it, Honey*, the wife said to her husband, *so that we can rescue it and take it home*. My wife and I looked at one another, thinking that she was joking. But the husband looked around, pointed to a peach basket with some towels in it, and asked us if he could borrow it. Tying together about fifty feet of baling twine left over from broken-open hay bales, the husband laid the string from the barn door where we sat out to a spot in the dirt where he spread a little of the horse-feed grain. He then turned the peach basket upside down over half of the grain and propped up one edge of the basket with a little stick tied to the string. He then walked back, sat down by us again, and resumed his stories, as we watched the peach basket. Sure enough, within a short while, the parakeet flittered down to peck at the grain. The wife hushed her husband, pointing toward the grain. The husband slowly reached for the string at his feet, gave it a quick tug, and a few seconds later had the parakeet in hand from under the peach basket, a parakeet that would now survive the coming winter because of the wife's importuning. My wife learned that fairy-tale bird-catching skill because she can walk quietly up to a fluttering bird trapped in our garage and catch it with her hands. She reminds me of Snow White when she walks the bird outside, opens her hand, and tosses it gently off into the air.

We also had training clients whose family and children were heavily involved in Arabian horses. One such client was the owner of the imported dark-liver stallion that dumped me on the racetrack, as mentioned above. The owner was a respected physician and equally respected family man and horse breeder who, like the stallion that he had me train, had come into the country from Poland. Hence, his interest in breeding Polish Arabians, although Polish Arabians were the top performance line anyway and also outstanding halter horses. His several children rode and showed prolifically, so his only need for training services was when he had a special-enough breeding horse to warrant sending the horse to a trainer for a potential big win. He sent horses to several different trainers, sending me only the stallion that dumped me, which I much appreciated nonetheless. Having the stallion was fun for the short while it lasted. I not only rode the stallion but also broke him to drive and showed him in driving, which I believe was the main purpose for which the owner had sent him to me. I had a similar opportunity with another family owner, this one a podiatrist whose son grew up to train professionally. Before the son had learned the skill, though, the owner father sent me a nice filly to show at halter and driving, and under saddle, at the state Futurity, where she won the saddle class. The podiatrist, a big fun-loving figure when at the shows, had a very nice stable the entrance to which he had decorated with big game that he had shot all over the world. Go figure.

I mention the owner who meant the most to my wife and I at the end of the book, but the schoolteacher and pig farmer couple from whom we bought Sam and Shani, as mentioned in an above chapter, were other great clients. They were a little different from many of our clients in that they managed their horse interest more like a business than a hobby, ambition, or recreational or sporting pursuit. Maybe it was because of the hogs, which to them were even more clearly a business rather than any kind of recreational pursuit. Hogs and horses seemed sometimes to run together for them, literally in the pastures and figuratively in their livestock business. Although they loved their horses and also had some fun with their hogs, they were not greatly sentimental about their horses, like other owners tended to be sentimental. They didn't invest their identities, whether masculinity, femininity, athleticism, ferociousness, or beauty, in their horses, as some and perhaps many owners did. They were thus great judges of the quality of their horses. Nothing much impressed or fooled them, which was a refreshing perspective in a horse world that was a lot about myth and glitter. I learned something from them every time we visited their farm to pick up, deliver, or evaluate a horse for them, just as I could see my wife doing. I think that we both learned more about life from them than we did from many other owners. Incredibly for a couple to whom each dollar meant something, they also once blessed us with a year-end bonus for training, which I don't recall other owners doing, as generous as were our other owners.

My wife and I also benefited greatly from training for another owner/breeder who treated her horse interest more like a business than a hobby, in her case out of both necessity and ambition. This owner, a veteran who delivered mail for the Postal Service until her disability, had an incredible eye for horses and knowledge of their lineage. She also bred some outstanding horses including the aforementioned world-beating Bert. We trained and showed for her a beautiful dark-bay stallion, winning halter championships and taking him to the National Championships where he did well making a first cut. The owner did quite a bit of breeding with the stallion as a result, much more than paying for the cost of training. Yet as skilled and successful as she was as a breeder and owner, she didn't have the wherewithal to look successful or, perhaps, just didn't care to do so. Her farm was an old hodgepodge of tiny buildings and muddy paddocks with horses here and there. She and her husband, whose only pursuit seemed to be keeping a private plane on a nearby field runway, lived in an old farmhouse so ramshackle that she would staple cardboard boot boxes to the interior walls to cover the holes and keep the cold wind out. They kept nothing in the refrigerator other than beer and horse medicine. Hilariously, when her husband cut wood in the winter to heat the house, he did so using a chainsaw *in the living room* to avoid the worst of the cold, throwing the cut wood chunks out the open front window into a big pile near the wood burner. For her part, the horse-owner wife wore an old jean jacket that she admitted she had spotted on and picked up from the highway like roadkill. Now that was a unique couple.

    My wife and I also served one other class of clientele, families with children who wanted to learn to ride and show. Serving these clients was a special ministry in supporting the children's education and maturation. Riding horses takes courage, athleticism, toughness, balance, coordination, consistency, and discipline, all attributes of which most of us would like more. Parents correctly see horseback riding as increasing their children's gifts in all these areas while bolstering the child's overall resilience. Riding horses also takes time, of which teenage children have way too much, in the view of some parents. Devoting one's teen years to a difficult but rewarding physical pursuit like horseback riding is far better in some parents' view than letting them play video games and absorb social media. And the benefit is not just from the riding. Horses require food, water, grooming, fresh air, exercise, and clean stalls, the provision for which takes additional teenager time and healthy labor. Better to serve another than to pursue one's own, even if the other whom one serves is a horse. My wife and I each spent countless hours caring for horses when in our teens, and when later training professionally, we were glad to help other teens and children do so. Working with families and their children also kept the training more of a sport and recreation than a service solely to businesses and investors.

One family of five headed by a school-counselor father and nurse mother was a prime example. The mother and oldest daughter especially loved horses. They bought from my mentor trainer the golden-colored three-year-old stallion (gelded by the time of their purchase) that I had unwittingly broke to saddle in a crash-test ride. The gelding at first seemed a challenging fit for the daughter because of the gelding's large size, natural strength, and unhandled spookiness. He was at raw talent, when the talent wasn't yet especially evident because of the rawness. But with perseverance on the part of the mother, daughter, trainer (me), and trainer's wife, who especially supported the family, the daughter and gelding made a strong and well-fit performance team. The tall and elegant daughter proved to have more mettle than some trainers. Indeed, if the family had bought a more-settled mount, of which they could have found plenty, the daughter would not have faced nearly so many worthwhile challenges as those that she eventually conquered. In choosing and caring deeply for the spooky gelding, they also turned a half-wild animal into a fully domesticated, gentle, reliable, and nurturing mount that the younger daughters were also able to ride and handle, an invaluable lesson in rescuing the lost.

My personal all-time favorite owner, though, was my wife. Like the family just mentioned, my wife (before we married) bought from my mentor trainer one of that bunch of half-wild horses that he had purchased and kept in the old barn across the road. In her case, my soon-to-be bride purchased a sweet, sixteen-hand light-bay three-year-old gelding, one that someone, presumably one of us at the trainer's farm, had already broken to saddle. The sweet gelding, though, hadn't yet learned the finer points of carrying a rider. His large size and youthful awkwardness combined to make him a challenging ride, not that he resented and might attempt to unseat a rider (he was too sweet for that) but that he galloped and galumphed more than cantered and just generally moved about like an awkward teenager. Hoping to show ride the gelding that next summer, my wife asked my mentor trainer if he or someone he knew could help her more-swiftly advance the gelding's training. He recommended me, of all persons. My wife and I first met briefly at a show held at a racetrack. Though she may correct me, I recall being in the ring in a halter class, advancing slowly up the line of horses waiting for the judge, when from the adjacent grandstand the father of a family with whom she had traveled to the show introduced us. Not too long later, she brought her tall, awkward but sweet gelding to my parents' farm where I was training.

As you might imagine from our marriage not long later, I took great interest in her gelding's swift advance to ensure that I would satisfy its special owner. Fortunately, the gelding was at just the right point in his development to make that advance. My wife had already put some good lunging and riding miles on the horse, laying just enough muscle across his formerly reedy frame for him to do more than he had so far exhibited. Although my first time on him made me wonder if he'd ever be able to do anything other than gallop awkwardly in a few long strides across the indoor arena, he surprised me how quickly he gathered himself into a fun, controlled ride. By the time my wife visited well into the one month that I expected to have him, the tall, sweet gelding was already doing turns on the haunches, shoulder outs and shoulder ins at the walk and trot, a little two-tracking across the arena's diagonals, and, most impressively, a canter so high, slow, and balanced that one could just about walk alongside him as he danced delicately around the arena. The young owner who would soon be my wife was pleased, which made me even happier. I don't think the future would have been any different for my wife and me together if the sweet gelding hadn't taken so swiftly and compliantly to my training, but I am eternally grateful that I never had to find out. God made me to serve my wife then and now, just as faith is receiving God's substance.

8

Breeders

A distinction exists between owning horses and being a horse breeder. Plenty of owners breed their horses. Owning a mare that then has a foal is an exciting, fun, and fascinating process. I bred my first horse, a little bay grade mare that had a little chestnut filly, soon selling the mare and filly to a nearby family. Following the little mare's gestation, attending to its foaling, and then helping to raise the foal was a remarkably tender experience. Read in a following chapter about breeding itself and about foaling. Yet breeding a horse or two and having an occasional foal to raise and sell isn't the same as being a breeder. Plenty of horse owners have the ambition to be breeders and even style themselves as such simply because they breed, foal, and raise horses. But a breeder is something different, someone whose research, keen horse eye, foresight, insight, resources, good fortune, and long-run perseverance make a mark on the breed, leaving a legacy in the precious gene pool. Anyone can breed horses. Few are true breeders. Trainers may be the stars of horse world, but breeders are the royalty. Ten trainers come and go, maybe even twenty or thirty, for one good breeder.

A large part of the challenge of breeding is that you don't always get what you want, even when you pay for it. Gene combinations are a funny thing. Just as is true for human siblings, equine full brothers and full sisters can be nearly as different in qualities as night and day. Just because a combination of sire to dam worked once doesn't mean that it will work again. Just because a horse is itself fast, strong, agile, straight-legged, or fine in features doesn't mean that it will reproduce those features. The stable at which we boarded our horses when we had a public-training stable had one of the very first offspring of the greatest racehorses of all time, Secretariat. As is traditional for premier racing stallions, Secretariat had at just two years old bred a couple of ordinary mares, in the case of this horse's dam not even a Thoroughbred like Secretariat but instead a draft horse. The great horse's draft-horse offspring was very ordinary, as it turned out most of Secretariat's offspring out of the finest Thoroughbred mares were also ordinary. Special horses can reproduce ordinary offspring and, to a degree, vice versa.

Breeding is thus more than a bit of a crap shoot. Sometimes, one gets the best attributes of both sire and dam. Other times, one gets the worst attributes of both. Usually, you get some of the good and some of the bad attributes. Yet even when sire and dam have only the best attributes, the offspring may somehow draw hidden bad attributes out of sire-and-dam recessive genes. Given the gross uncertainty, then, what keeps breeders coming back? In relative terms, stud fees are not that expensive. Oh, sure, stud fees for the very best stallions may be substantial, but stud fees for very good stallions, far better than the breeder's mares, can be quite reasonable. Breeders face the lure of nearly always breeding above, and often well above, their mares' value, suggesting swift improvement in a lower-valued mare's modest attributes. In theory, every equine generation should be better because of the selective possibilities in having a few great stallions breeding many ordinary mares. And the real magic, the real gamble that keeps breeders coming back after myriad disappointments? Sometimes, breeding to the typically better stallion somehow draws hidden good attributes out of an ordinary mare or hidden superb attributes out of a good mare. Once in a great while, breeding produces a shooting star, a glorious genetic anomaly.

When it comes to reproducing equine offspring, breeders usually much prefer fillies over colts, for reasons suggested just above. Unless a colt is far superior to other colts, like a top five percenter, fillies fetch substantially higher prices than colts fetch because purchasers can soon breed the fillies, as mature mares, to superior stallions, in theory reproducing ever more-valuable offspring. A breeder has little to no use for colts born of the breeder's dominant stallion, even the few very special colts worth keeping for breeding, because the breeder could not breed the colt to any of its many sibling fillies. And unless a colt is destined for stud, meaning in the top five or ten percent of all colts, a purchaser has only one use for it, which would be as a recreational-use gelding. Despite their great utility for recreational purposes, geldings are ordinarily a lot cheaper than mares because of their inability to reproduce. And so again, when a mare gives birth to a filly, the breeder celebrates, while when a mare gives birth to a colt, the breeder weeps. Because breeders celebrate or weep over the sex of each newborn foal, breeders were often looking for something, anything, to improve the fifty-fifty odds. Some followed moon-and-tide charts—no kidding. Others had other odd theories complicating the already-complicated process of ensuring a timely and therefore successful breeding.

Becoming a successful breeder also involves a balancing act between aggressive marketing and selling of stud services and offspring, combined with a strong proprietary sense to preserve the influential core of the gene pool by not selling off the best breeding stock. Breeders who keep and breed their own mares, which is most breeders, must sell at least some offspring to cull the growing herd. Buyers, of course, want to buy the best rather than the worst offspring. But breeders must protect their own farm's gene pool and so cannot sell the best without risking diluting the precious genes and their ability to maintain and improve the future horse stock. Thus, every breeding farm has its untouchable horses, some young, some prime, and some old. Buyers come to the farm, salivate over the unavailable core stock, and walk away with the castoffs, hoping that they have outwitted the breeder with a diamond in the rough. Breeders must thus be masters of mirrors, able to sell the mystique of the farm without giving away anything other than castoffs. Here's a tip: don't buy from a breeder. You'll pay through the nose and be disappointed. Instead, send the best mare that you can find and afford to the breeder's best stallion, and hope for your own comet.

Through fortune more than anything (certainly not through influence), I met several of the Arabian breeds most-prominent breeders. My wife and I delivered a couple of mares to a famous Egyptian-Arabian breeder's farm in Texas, to breed to one of the breeder's best stallions. It turned out to be one of those trips where everything that could go wrong did go wrong. First, we had a flat tire on the way down, necessitating pulling over on the shoulder of the freeway and waiting for help. The help came too late to finish the trip that day, and so we found a nearby old farm in which to stable the two mares overnight. Unfortunately, the kind farm owner decided after we left for a hotel to take the halter off one of the two horses, a horse that we were delivering for someone else and whose owner warned us *not* to remove the halter or we'd never get it back on. The next morning, trailer tire repaired, we struggled mightily to get the halter back on the mare before loading, once again delaying the trip. To make matters worse, as we approached our destination, rain came down harder than I've ever seen it rain, slowing our trip to a crawl. By the time we got to Texas, it was the middle of the night. Then we learned from a sleepy farmhand awaiting our arrival that the breeder didn't let any outside horses on her farm and that we had to take the horses to a nearby destination. Off we went again.

We got to meet the breeder the next day, one of the more curious figures in the breed. Her husband was an oilman out of whose wealth she had initially built her Egyptian breeding stock. Wealth alone does not a breeder make. Plenty of rich folks have spent fortunes in horses and come up with just about nothing. This breeder, though, clearly had an eye for horses. A few National Champions later, she didn't need her husband's wealth to pay for maintaining the breeding stock. Her eye, though, was only part of the equation. The breeder also had an affinity for things Egyptian, meaning not just the horses but also the people, history, culture, and furnishings, all of which was wise and is admirable. Her knowledge and affinity had helped her buy Egyptian horse stock from the Egyptian government to import from Cairo to Texas, despite that the Egyptian government, which owned the best Arabians in that country, is just as protective of its gene pool as any other breeder would be. All that makes sense, but the curious part about this breeder was that in Texas and at horse shows around the country, she tended to dress, make herself up, and even to act Egyptian, looking among the Egyptian furniture and artifacts around her stable and home, like a demure or regal modern-day Cleopatra, or so it looked and seemed to me, a Midwestern rube. I didn't know her well enough to determine if it was just good marketing or true affinity, but she did cut a mysterious figure.

That breeder fit one of two molds that one finds among breeders. Some, like the Egyptian breeder, appear true believers whose whole lives they wrap up in the history and preservation of the peculiar strain that they pursue, to the point of taking on the strain's identity. I visited another such breeder, this one hidden in a spectacular valley in mountains north of Santa Fe, New Mexico, to pick up a stallion of a rare imported-Arabian strain, that a client had purchased and asked me to retrieve and train. The valley breeder had more of this especially rare strain of horses than anyone else in the country. Indeed, the breeder had the reputation of having preserved from extinction the purity and existence of this rare strain. From the reverence with which my client and others described the strain and its preservationist breeder, I expected something special. The farm, although in one of the most dramatic and beautiful valleys I have ever seen, was instead ramshackle, a few tiny falling-down barns surrounded by tiny wire-encircled pens. To my shock, the horses were no better, so small and unhealthy looking as to clearly be the product of severe inbreeding, which their pedigrees confirmed. I would not have wanted one of them, despite their rarity and strange acclaim. Purity has its drawbacks. Crossbreeding produces the stars.

The other kind of breeder that one finds is the conqueror, the one who has already made or inherited zillions, is already powerful through riches, position, or influence, and pursues horse breeding to reflect and amplify that power. Arabian horses in the desert were important instruments of war but also totems of wealth, power, and status. Arabian horses in modern society are only the latter, not the former, but can still be significant symbols, given as gifts or sold as prizes to those whose relationship the powerful value. The breeder for whom my mentor trained may have been a suitable example. His automotive-industry wealth and willingness to pursue horse-world connections enabled him to acquire, breed, and show a string of wonderful performance and halter champions. Yet as wonderful as they were, he promptly sold them all at a spectacular auction in order to purchase and import seventeen Egyptian Arabians from the government in Cairo. He then repeated his former feat, breeding and showing a solid string of champions including winning National Championships with his new strain. He didn't appear soaked in Egyptian culture, like the Texas breeder. He seemed to have just seen something exciting and challenging to do within his reach and then went out and did it, much to the credit of his business and network acumen. A Midwest trucking company magnate was a similar Arab breeder, although of an early domestic strain, who relocated his breeding operation to Scottsdale before the city became Arabian horse world's mecca.

Entertainers who have bred Arabians, like the Las Vegas entertainer Wayne Newton and the Broadway playwright and producer Mike Nichols, may have done so less out of ambition to make a mark and leave a legacy, or for influence, than out of their aesthetic appreciation. Owning the finest Arabians is a bit like owning painting or sculpture masterpieces, except the horses live, breathe, prance, parade, and reproduce. Wayne Newton bred and raised some beautiful white Arabians, although he wasn't as successful a breeder as Mike Nichols, who bred and had his trainer show some of the most exquisite halter and performance National Champions. Mr. Nichols' sensitivity for his Broadway performance art somehow translated into sensibility for fine Arabians. He even mixed his two passions in a theater-like sale of dozens of his horses at his own farm. My wife and I, and just about every other Arabian enthusiast, fell in love with an imported National Champion mare of his that was so fine and delicate, long and lanky, straight and sound, and effortlessly graceful that the mare left the mesmerizing effect of a runway model. One knew that one could not handle, show, ride, breed, or acquire an ownership interest in her but could instead only admire her from afar, which made her presence at a major show all the more seductive.

Breeders of any type must think about their legacy. Horses reproduce slowly and live relatively long reproductive lives. Breeders make progress in shaping a line or breed only slowly, over substantial time. But then, what one does over that long haul will itself have a long-term impact on future generations of horses and breeders. My family bought a horse from a second-generation breeder whom we got to know some. Her parents had preserved and developed an important line of early Arabians imported from England, breeding National Champions in both halter and performance before other breeders started importing fresh lines of Polish, Egyptian, Spanish, and other Arabian horses from around the world. At one time, this second-generation breeder's parents were the best breeders around. They had succeeded in passing to their breeder daughter an important domestic bloodstock on which she could draw for her own breeding plans. Yet the bloodstock clearly needed refreshing rather than further interbreeding. Which way to go was the question, not whether to preserve a pure old-fashioned line. The breeder daughter, though, married a horseman from another breed, and while the marriage was a success, the breeder daughter lost the vision. Before long, the imports and powerful interbreeding of different strains had produced horses so far superior to the old bloodstock that time had passed it by, leaving herds of old mares standing barren and idle, waiting to live out their dying line. My wife and I got to know another older breeder couple and their adult daughter, whose breeding stock suffered a similar fate. Time doesn't stand still, even for horses. If you are not improving your bloodstock, then you are dooming its line.

Regional breeders can also have success. My wife and I got to know and thoroughly enjoy a breeder who had a blood-red-bay stallion that no one could beat in local competitions, even though the stallion wouldn't prevail in statewide or national competition. The breeder, a pawn-shop owner by day (of all things), had several decent mares of his own, which he kept bred to his stallion, producing solid, even talented offspring that easily won locally and even had some statewide success. The stallion's home-bred success attracted outside mares, earning the breeder solid income in reasonably priced stud fees. After many good years of such success, though, the breeder faced a crossroads. He now had female offspring of his stallion needing their own breeding, as did some of the owners who had sent mares to his stallion. One doesn't breed a stallion to its own daughter. Breeders rarely breed sibling offspring to preserve the common sire's influence but always at the risk of the stunted-inbred curse. Ultimately, a breeder's challenge is how to selectively reach outside of the favored bloodline for fresh lineage that will both carry the original line forward but also freshen and improve it. Wisely, this regional breeder, who was not about strains or purity but instead about owning and breeding special horses, started experimenting with cautious outcrosses and to some good early effect. Oh, and our enjoyment of the breeder? He liked to throw home parties where everyone gathered in his cozy playroom for clean-fun games late into the weekend night, where the talk was all horses.

Ultimately, breeders who breed to compete and compete to breed, like the salt-of-the-earth pawn-shop-owner breeder, save a breed. Competition proves the merit of the breeding. Breeding is so time and resource consuming that one can get lost in one's own bloodline and in doing so lose sight of the breed standard. Competition quickly sets one aright. If one's neighbor's horse has straighter legs, longer neck, greater angle to the shoulder, stronger and flatter croup, higher performance action, and prettier head, then the competition win proves it better bred, no matter how famous or obscure its bloodlines. Shows are great levelers. Breeders can take all the pride that they wish in preserving bloodlines of famous ancestors, but preservation of lineage is not the goal. It didn't work for English kings or other human royalty and doesn't work for horses. The goal is to breed, show, and share horses so beautiful, powerful, and graceful that they take your breath away, making you want to disappear in timeless marvel. Breeders can do that when they look away from the names, places of origin, and reputations to the horses themselves. Ultimately, horses don't succeed or fail on the reputation of their sire or dam, just like we don't succeed or fail on the reputation of momma or poppa. Each horse makes its own way, just as we must do.

9

Grooms

If trainers are horse world's engines, breeders supply the vehicles, and owners supply the gas, then grooms are the wheels, keeping the whole affair on the road. Horse world would get nowhere without them. Grooms are the lower-cost labor that enables trainers to employ their higher-cost skills. Little gets done in a training stable without a groom. Simply caring for the horses soaks up hour after hour, leaving only spare minutes for the training. A task so seemingly simple as watering the horses can take laying out and rolling up hoses or lugging heavy bucket after heavy bucket, retrieving and fixing the empty rubber water buckets that the horses have torn from their stable wall, and dumping and scrubbing buckets that the horses have filled with feed, hay, or worse. Grinding, mixing, supplementing, and feeding grain to the horses two or three times a day becomes a similarly complex operation, while filling hay racks or untying, filling, and retying hay bags is another twice-a-day chore. Then the stalls need cleaning, which means not only removing the soiled shavings or straw using pitchfork or shovel but also replacing it with fresh bedding, not to mention moving the horses out of the way from stall to stall or outdoors to do so. Only then can one begin to think about the exercise and training aspects.

Grooms are no less essential for efficient training. When a trainer is ready to train a horse, the horse could be anywhere around the farm, whether conveniently in a nearby stall or instead out in a paddock, shed, or distant barn or pasture. Simply retrieving the horse for a workout can take precious minutes. Every horse then needs some basic grooming before training, things like brushing off whatever dirt, shavings, or straw the horse has all over it before the surcingle or saddle goes on, untangling the horse's mane, tail, and forelock, and picking the packed dirt and stones out of the horse's four hooves. Basic grooming can further include tending the splints, sores, and contusions that horses naturally acquire and then laboriously wrapping legs and ankles and booting hooves to avoid further nicks and problem lameness. Wrapping or re-wrapping the long-flowing tail to preserve its length can alone add minutes to the labors. Only then can the groom retrieve the necessary tack possibly including bridle, bit, reins or side reins, lunge line or driving lines, surcingle or saddle, girth, and sweat hood, and fit it all to the horse, one hopes with the horse cooperating. The process of preparing a horse for a training workout can take fifteen or twenty minutes, making a groom essential to the trainer's efficient use of limited time. The groom prepares the next horse while the trainer trains the first one.

More groom's work remains when the trainer is done training the horse. The groom must remove the tack from the sweating or even lathered-up horse, sponge wipe or hose off the sweat and lather, and cool down the horse with a slow hand walk or by clipping it to a mechanical horse walker. Proper cooling off can take up to twenty or thirty minutes of walking. Failing to cool off the horse can lead to heat retained in the hooves and permanently disabling laminitis. A groom has full hands between getting the next horse ready for training and cooling off the horse already worked. A trainer can easily keep one groom very busy or two grooms busy enough, depending on each workout's length and intensity, from as little as fifteen or twenty minutes to as much as forty-five minutes or an hour. Trainers may also have grooms handle some of the workouts, especially simple line lunging or free lunging of horses for aerobic exercise but also anaerobic exercise on a steep treadmill. Trainers tend to drop in for four to six hours of training eight to ten horses after grooms have fed and watered the horses and cleaned stalls, after which grooms have once again to feed and water. Grooms may thus work many more hours at the stables than do trainers, although trainers have many other business-development and management responsibilities that grooms do not have.

Grooms, though, are much more than just labor. They also establish or heavily influence the character and spirit of the stables. The trainer may be in good mood or bad, certainly having its effect. A cheerful, friendly, sensitive, generous, and confident trainer can buoy not only owners but also grooms. Yet the constant presence and unending activity of the grooms in and around the stable give the stable its temperament. Grooms are often young and carefree, especially the high school students that trainers employ in the summers at shows, for whom getting paid to live away from home and travel has a natural attraction, before the reality of a lifetime of work and adult responsibility sinks in. Our favorite groom Keith fell into this category. Keith was a tall, lanky, and happy-go-lucky teenage son of a police-chief father and office-manager mother. His parents had the good sense to tempt him with a horse-training vocation rather than let him waste his natural exuberance on traditional and less-healthy teenage pursuits. Grooming was his entrée to the training profession, although he had a good way yet to go to reach that goal, given a recent growth spurt and his typical teenage clumsiness.

For a time, Keith went everywhere with us. Not only did he work summers with me at the stable where I trained, helping me by saddling, unsaddling, and cooling out horse after horse, for the observation and occasional ride in between, and also traveled to all the summer shows with us, but Keith also took off high school for up to a month at a time to travel with us to early or late-season shows out of state. Keith went to New Jersey, Delaware, Toronto, Columbus, Miami, Tampa, Indianapolis, Springfield, and Louisville with us, among many other places. I would have accomplished a fraction of what I did but for Keith's steady and always good-natured help. An example of both Keith's unflagging good spirits and his Keystone Cops clumsiness occurred just before our first of three shows in Florida one November. We drove two very long days from Michigan, stopping only for a brief overnight at a Georgia farm, before arriving late night at Miami's Hialeah Racetrack. The three-day show there was to take place after a few furious days of clipping, working, bathing, and show-grooming the eight or so horses we had taken with us. Somewhere in that frantic work, Keith was cleaning a stall the horse occupant of which bumped the handle of his shovel into Keith's nose, obviously breaking it given that it now had a distinct curve to one side.

My wife and I had married just a couple of months before and, at ages twenty and twenty-one, were ourselves not much more mature than the awkward teenager Keith whose charge, broken nose and all, we now had. Off we went in the big pickup truck through the strange streets of Miami, looking for an emergency room, while Keith good-naturedly held a towel to his bleeding nose, trying hard not to laugh at the emerging situation his clumsiness had created. We finally found a hospital that would help. After a little while, Keith sat on the examination table as we listened to the doctor explain what it meant for the radiograph to have confirmed that Keith had indeed broken his nose, justifying its misalignment. The doctor thought it best to just push Keith's nose back into alignment and hope to leave it at that, if Keith could just avoid knocking it back out of alignment again until it could heal sometime in the next couple of months. With little other choice, we agreed that the doctor should give it a try, which he did with his hands placed on Keith's forehead with one thumb on either side of his nose to try to get the alignment just right. The doctor stared at Keith's nose as Keith stared firmly back into the doctor's eyes, trying not to either laugh or cry, both of which he badly wanted to do. We were on our way back to the racetrack a few minutes later with a great story to tell but a lot more work yet to get done.

Poignantly, a couple decades later my wife and I lent our teenage daughter for a week as an extra groom for Keith, to help his other grooms prepare for a show, when Keith was a big-time trainer. Our daughter had a great time, coming home as exhausted and dirty as a teenager can get doing anything so healthy. She had no more energy left at night from the long day's grooming work than to fall into bed at the nearby room another groom lent her, to sleep with her clothes on. Our daughter had only irregular prior experiences with horses, hanging out at a farm owned by my wife's friends, not the years of full-time horse work that my wife and I had shared. Yet Keith and his regular grooms cared for her so well that she came home feeling grown up and accomplished, another debt we owe to Keith. She told us great stories of free lunging horses, chasing them around the arena with a bleach bottle filled with rocks, and endless clipping and bathing.

Keith and the other young grooms we employed generally worked so hard and were so precious to us that we tried, when at long shows or on the road between them, to do more than just wear them out bathing and grooming horses. Of course, we tried to feed them well, not just with fairgrounds food but occasionally with good meals at decent restaurants. Those meals were when the natural tension of the show's hard work and up-and-down competitions eased, and the good stories and great laughter came out. The fairgrounds, arenas, and racetracks where we showed sometimes afforded the grooms happy diversions like motorcycle races, carnival midways, and amusement rides. Elvis performed on the fairgrounds of one show in Louisville when we were there. We heard the famous announcement that he had left the building, just as his bus passed through the barn area on the way out a back gate. The show grounds tended to be not in the best part of town. For safe diversions, we were mostly stuck to the fairgrounds unless we could plan a trip to another part of town. In Springfield, we took the grooms to the fascinating Lincoln Presidential Museum. In Miami, we searched fruitlessly for a public beach.

Grooms, though, are not always happy-go-lucky high school students. They may also be wary high school graduates or dropouts for whom college lies beyond interest or reach, a lifetime of work in the stables seeming then like an increasingly heavy chore. A few older grooms nonetheless make a career of it, perhaps following an unsuccessful attempt to attain the status and income of a trainer or as adjunct to managing a farm. The manager of the stable at which my wife and I boarded our clients' horses employed an older groom, a hardworking but quiet, brooding fellow who lived alone in the old farmhouse across the dirt road from the stable and naturally kept to himself. For a time, he made keeping to himself much easier by ingesting great quantities of medicinal garlic the stench of which followed him through the barns as he cleaned stalls and fed and watered horses, until complaints from the boarders eventually forced his employer to make him stop. Keeping to yourself is one thing, while causing the boarders to flee the barn for fresh air is quite another.

My parents also employed an older groom who then served as farm manager and even showed some horses after my wife and I left the farm. I had worked with the older groom at my mentor's farm, from which my parents recruited him. He was a kindly older gentleman whose whole life he had devoted to the care of horses. He knew quite a bit about home remedies yet surprisingly had little reliable horse sense, surviving only with angels looking out for him. When we would breed horses, which was nearly every other day throughout the spring, we always tried to give him the thankless but safer job of holding the mare, not the much-more-dangerous and more-critical job of handling the stallion. He wisely took to wearing a little white Red Cross army helmet the few times that he did handle the stallion because he would foolishly stand right under the stallion as it reared and struck with its hooves over his head. The sensible thing to do when a horse rears is to step back to the end of the lead line, holding the lead as high aloft as one's arm can take it, so that you neither get clobbered with the rearing horse's flailing front hooves nor allow the horse to get a leg over the lead line, which means losing control of the horse when it comes back down from its rear. Despite our warning, this kindly older groom would instead try to hold the stallion down from its rear, an impossible attempt, by standing directly under it while pulling down on the lead line. The stallion would inevitably come down from its rear with a leg over the line, enabling the stallion to run off free after the mare and its now-helpless handler. Roaring, kicking, dangerous chaos ensued.

Spouses, children, other family members, and friends of trainers also often serve as grooms, at least in a substitute or temporary capacity, although sometimes also in more-permanent roles. The trainer couple mentioned in a prior chapter, who befriended and mentored my wife and me, had that symbiotic relationship with the husband riding and training the horses while the wife groomed, bathed, tacked, and untacked them, one after another. They worked like clockwork together training at home, until their school-age daughters joined them to help their mother groom at the shows. Their free or low-cost family labor was one reason why they did so well financially, able to afford better riding suits, boots, and hats, and even a sports car (used, but still a sports car) that the husband had always wanted, beyond the requisite trailer-hauling pickup truck. My wife did tons of grooming for me at home and quite a bit at shows, too, and I a little for her, although we tried at shows to always have a groom around like the invaluable Keith.

As hardworking and essential as grooms are to horse trainers, most trainers at one time or another have done everything that a groom will do. Even though I tried to spend my time training, as trainers must, I probably did, and other trainers over a lifetime probably also do, more total hours of other work, like feeding and watering horses, cleaning stalls, spreading manure on the pastures, moving horses to and from pastures, and fixing stalls and fences. I also did a little grooming work for others. While most of my work for my mentor trainer was as an apprentice trainer, meaning that I rode and ground-worked horses rather than cleaned stalls and bathed horses, I also served him on rare occasion in a mixed role of apprentice and groom, when he and I would head across country for an exhibition or small show with only a couple or handful of horses rather than a full contingent of eight or ten horses for a National Championship or major show. At those small events, he too would share in the little grooming work, which wasn't unusual that a trainer would clip and bathe a horse or clean a stall or two. The rule is generally *all hands on deck* when one has so much work to do. In a running joke that we had, my wife would even sometimes pay me to go feed, water, and turn out the horses on Sunday mornings when it was officially her turn but she was especially tired, the joke of course being that no money exchanged hands, which was all our shared money in any case. I never regretted assuming her Sunday-morning turn, as hard as she worked for us. Better to receive her abundant grace at the cost of a little self-interest.

10

Grooming

Basic grooming is a big part of owning a horse and, in its own way, one of the better parts of ownership. Knocking dirt, chaff, and dried mud off a horse with a wood-handled stiff-straw brush, and picking the packed dirt out of its hooves with a metal hoof pick, has something timeless about it. Horse owners must have been doing such grooming for thousands of years, probably the first equine/human activity before full domestication and any productive use. Horses having had regular brushing learn to relish it, like dogs enjoy stroking. Find just the right spot, often at the base of the crest of the horse's neck or about the horse's withers, and the horse will raise its poll, twist its mouth, and lean into the scratching, rubbing, and brushing. If you put your hand in front of the horse's mouth while scratching its withers, then sometimes it will wiggle its muzzle in your palm, emulating your scratching, as pastured horses sometimes scratch one another simultaneously in equine evidence of the saying *you scratch my back and I'll scratch yours*. Rubber or steel curry combs and steel shedding blades are especially effective grooming tools in spring when the horses shed their thick winter coats. A horse that receives good nutrition, some exercise, and lots of currying, can develop a beautifully tight and glistening coat. Regular vacuuming with a special horse vacuum adds to the impressive glisten. To learn more about stock-horse training (ride 'em and slide 'em), I spent a few days working for a Quarter Horse trainer and draft-horse owner who spent hours currying and vacuuming his horses. I'd never seen such beautiful horse coats.

Another basic grooming that any horse needs is to untangle mane and tail. Manes and tails have definite function in keeping away biting flies, especially the huge horse flies and small deer flies that chase and plague horses in mid-to-late summer. Horses use their tails to flick flies away, while the mane serves a similar function. We once had a stallion get a horse-fly bite right on the croup where the tail couldn't quite reach it. The bite somehow got badly infected, later bursting into an open three-inch abscess that we had to cover for the rest of the summer as it healed. Pastured horses, though, pick up burrs, twigs, and tangles in the mane and tail so that, without regular care, the mane and tail become dreadlocks. Untangling dreadlocks can be an hours-long process, especially when knotted together by the infamous burdock, which sticks more quickly and stronger than Velcro. Combs and brushes don't work. You must hold the burr while painstakingly pulling out hair by hair. If you find any burdock in your pasture, then cut it down and burn it so that the seeds don't spread, or you'll forever regret it. Such is temptation's nature, tangled by a single burr.

The show grooming of an Arabian horse and most other show horses is a subject unto itself. The prior chapter's brief mention of the things that grooms do to prepare a horse to show, like to clip and bathe a horse, barely begins to describe the efforts to which grooms will go to make their horse look better than other horses in the competition. Arabians are supposed to be among the more natural of breeds. Their owners do not, for instance, cut and set an Arab's tail dock like a Saddlebred owner would do. Yet even with Arabs, grooms leave almost nothing to nature when it comes to preparing to show. The glamorous effect of their grooming labors can be stunning, certainly a difference maker in halter classes, especially when combined with a skilled trainer's way of standing up the horse for show. A well-groomed Arab prepared to show at halter by a top groom looks every bit as primped and primed as a Hollywood star walking the red carpet, where the stars and their hairdressers and makeup artists also leave nothing to nature. A very few stars may still look the part when they tumble wearily out of bed the next morning, but they all look glamorous on the red carpet. And so do well-groomed Arabs in the show ring.

Grooming changed a lot from when I started showing Arabs to when I finished a while later, owing entirely to the swift process of one competitor's grooming advances that took other competitors only a short while to discover and adopt. Tack-shop trailers that showed up at the bigger shows aided and abetted the disclosure of grooming secrets as they heard and responded to the whispered demand for new grooming products. Yet grooms employed by different trainers also shared or stole the secrets from one another. Grooms play and sometimes even party together late night at shows before falling asleep in their tack stalls, thus finding it hard to keep secrets from one another for long. A show season begins with one competitor having a grooming edge but ends with everyone sharing the same secret. One day a halter horse appears with an eye-catching new grooming twist, but by the next day ten horses wear the same style.

One of the big advances came in clipping horses. Horses in the wild have long hair in places that show horses don't need it, like chins, fetlocks, and bridle paths. At one time, every groom used the same kind of clipper and blade to shave the chin and chop away at the fetlocks, and to clip the long mane hair from the bridle path, no more than the couple of inches necessary to pass the show halter over it. Gradually, refinements came. The bridle paths got gradually longer, first four inches, then six, then ten or twelve inches, until the horses had only a vestige of mane remaining. The effect was to make the horse's neck look longer, a highly desirable trait. Soon, though, shaving the bridle paths and chins with the standard blades was no longer enough. The hair instead required an extremely close clip using a special blade. Then, shaving chin, bridle path, and fetlock wasn't enough. The whole horse needed clipping with a larger-size clipper, giving the full coat an especially sleek look. What had been a ten-minute clipping job now took hours of patient, itchy work to which some horses, especially the younger ones, did not take kindly. The body-clipped horse then needed to wear at least a blanket and, if the weather was chilly, also a hood to remain warm in the stall or pasture. At what cost, beauty?

What hair remained of the mane, forelock, and tail soon required its own special treatment. At one time, getting it clean with ordinary shampoo or maybe a special horse shampoo was sufficient. Then someone figured out how to get a white mane and tail truly white, using special whiteners, or black mane and tail truly black, with black dyes. Grooms then began wrapping tails up into little braided balls so that they could grow long and luxurious, indeed so long that the tail dragged on the ground behind the horse. Blowing the tail dry after washing, separating each strand from each strand, gave the tail fuller body to match its luxurious length, unless of course the owner wanted a slight wave in the tail hair, in which case the groom would give it a loose braid while still slightly damp. The groom would brush the primped tail out fully just before entering the ring but keep it tied in a loose knot until right at the ring gate so that it dragged along the ground only while showing. If the horse had white socks or blaze, then grooms might apply white powder to make them stand out brilliantly.

Grooms reserved the greatest effort, though, for preparing the horse's hooves for the show ring. Clean hooves, scrubbed with soap, water, and brush, was once sufficient. Then came hoof black, a lacquer applied with a sponge dauber from a small can to darken black hooves. Yet darker black hooves wasn't enough. Soon, grooms were sanding hooves to remove the natural lines and imperfections before applying the hoof black. Yet relatively smooth and relatively black hooves were soon not enough. Hooves needed sanding with finer-grit paper on a circular sander between multiple coats of hoof black and a final coat of shiny clear lacquer. Grooms would lift the horse's hoof up onto a stand or knee to smooth with an electric circular sander and then, after multiple applications of hoof black and coatings of clear, to buff out to a high gloss. You could see your reflection in the better-groomed hooves, like the highly finish on a fine motor vehicle's hood. Owners and trainers judged and valued grooms on the quality of the mirror finish to the hooves of the horses they groomed. The effect of all this grooming activity at the show barn gave it the atmosphere of an equine salon, treating both hair and nails, busy activity that could stretch from the early dawn to late at night.

Some of the newer aspects of grooming in an increasingly competitive horse-show environment were controversial, indeed real or technical violations of grooming rules. A keen offense involved applying ginger in brown paste form to irritate the skin below a halter horse's tail (to avoid more-accurate but less-pleasant location descriptors) so that the horse kept its tail up in the show ring. The practice was strictly against the rules but also one on which some owners insisted and other owners expected whether they said so or not. One owner would even make the offending ginger application herself if the groom and trainer were unavailable or unwilling. Interestingly, my mentor trainer showed a National Champion stallion that had an extraordinarily unusual, high-raised tail even when the stallion was entirely relaxed, no ginger application necessary. The tail stuck up like a little trailing flag not just when one paraded the stallion around in a ring but even when the stallion was relaxed back in the stall. I could vouch for its naturalness and genuineness, having worked around and schooled the stallion in my apprentice duties. The irony is that the trainer had to deliberately advertise that the stallion's unusual raised tail was natural and *not* ginger's product. Otherwise, the National Championship show judges might have penalized the trainer at the cost of a National Championship. Despite the trainer and owner making valiant advance efforts to discredit any rumors of ginger use, or perhaps because of their efforts, one of the National Championship show judges deliberately ran his hand over the stallion's croup and tail to see the tail's response and judge or prove to the crowd its naturalness. Cheating affects everyone, both guilty and innocent.

One may justly wonder what effect all the primping and pampering has on a horse. My mentor trainer taught me something hugely important that few other trainers and owners seemed to know. Horses need a certain degree of natural development just like other animals do. The strong temptation is to baby, pamper, and protect the best young horses from the bumps and bruises or, worse, injuries and scars of rugged outdoor life in a big pasture filled with bossy older and rambunctious younger horses. The temptation is to ensconce the emerging young stars in the best stalls in the heated stable rather than let them fend for themselves through a winter storm in an exposed paddock with a lean-to shelter. Simply showing a yearling or two-year-old horse requires quite a bit of sheltering and pampering. The problem is that without the invigorating outdoor air, open pasture, and cavorting exercise that a band of rowdy young horses will naturally engender, a young horse does not develop a healthy horse's bone, muscle, size, stamina, and character. Pampering produces hothouse horses, yes without blemish but also smaller, weaker, and less coordinated and athletic. They lose their imposing, impressive, awe-striking character as horses, once used for plowing and hauling and war, and instead take on the character of china dolls valuable only as collectibles.

My mentor trainer knew well the permanently disabling effects of the pampering phenomenon and did what he could to counteract it. When the owner of the Midwestern farm that he managed was away down South in the winter, the trainer would turn loose in paddocks and pastures every one of the stables most premier horses, letting them race and chase one another up and down the paddock fences, rear, spin, and race off again. The owner would have had a heart attack that these expensive collectibles were going to injure or scar themselves, which on occasion they did, although the injuries and scars generally healed, making the horse all the stronger and bolder. With his few own horses, the trainer refused any babying. They stayed outdoors across the road, running and grazing in large pastures, until the trainer wanted to use them or needed to sell them. I watched a colt of his, one for which he seemed to take no care whatsoever in its primitive conditions but was instead letting develop free and wild, grow into a mammoth and magnificent park horse, the most physically imposing Arab I ever saw. Raising the colt in the hothouse barn would have ruined him.

An owner for whom I worked made that mistake with his best colt, and I was unable to prevent it. He bred one of his better mares to a top stallion, the breeding producing a striking bay colt with a gorgeous head, nearly perfect conformation, and even a surprising degree of athleticism. Several show wins as a yearling proved the colt's superiority. The owner had us move him up into the best stall in the stable where the owner could show him off to every visitor. In the owner's view, the colt's frequent display and great value meant that we had to keep him groomed, clipped, blanketed, hooded, and safe, with his only exercise a few solitary minutes a day of getting chased around the indoor ring. He became a complete hothouse project, despite that the owner had reasonably secure paddocks and large rolling pastures where the colt could have run and competed with other colts, developing a horse's full frame and musculature, social instincts, and physiological attributes. He did very well as a yearling and early two-year-old, winning a high place at a national show across country, where the trainer for a prominent Arabian breeder took an interest in the colt. But the owner's insistence on protecting the colt from a horse's natural outdoor environment had already doomed the colt to underdevelopment. The colt was an afterthought before the end of his second year, a burned-out phenomenon that would never develop a horse's grace and athleticism, imposing character, or staunch frame.

As this lesson suggests, preparing champion Arabians for halter competition involves not just extraordinary grooming but also fitting the horse. One can make a surprising contribution to the natural arch of a horse's neck, for instance, with proper fitting. Arabians should have high-set necks with some crest (not thick like a Morgan Horse, but still a good crest) leading to a narrow throatlatch. Using bit, bridle, side reins, and surcingle to set the horse's forehead perpendicular to the ground as it walks, trots, and canters loose or on a lunge line tends to stretch and strengthen the crest while constraining and narrowing the throatlatch. A good bit of ground work of that kind will make the horse a stronger competitor at halter. Trainers will add a sweat hood (neoprene wrapped around the neck) during the workouts trying to reduce fat deposits on the neck. To muscle the hindquarters and level the croup to Arabian standards, trainers use treadmills or even swim the horse, as previously indicated. We used an adjustable treadmill to especially good effect. A few minutes for the horse to walk steeply uphill on the treadmill did wonders. In short, owners would spare little cost, and trainers would go to great lengths, to give the greatest boost to the horse's natural beauty.

Grooming and fitting efforts all came together when the professional photographer visited the farm. Horse photography is essential to a farm's marketing efforts. Show wins are great, but a full-page advertisement in the monthly Arabian horse magazine with a striking photograph of the champion could mean much more in promoting the sale of stud fees and offspring. A spectacular photograph could be worth far more to a stallion's owner than not only the proverbial thousand words but also a string of show victories. The premier photographers were thus much in demand, traveling the country from farm to farm on a schedule booked months in advance. The top two or three photographers were every bit as famous, sought-after, and expensive as the top trainers, stars with their own wide following. They were also entertainers, taking with them from farm to farm news and gossip that piqued the ears and fueled the ambitions of their hosts and employers who in return paid their substantial photography fees and first-class expenses. Indeed, owners and trainers treated the photographers like royalty so that they would carry good word of their horse stock, methods, skill, and character to their other destinations. Photographers could build or break reputations, not only by their camera angles, shutter timing, and studio touch-up skills but also by their word of mouth.

Show photography, consisting of a quick assembly-line shot of the blue-ribbon award in the show ring, could help promote a horse or trainer, but the valuable photography took place at the farm, where photographer, assistant, trainer, and grooms could work for hours to get a few good shots. All-day and even two-day photography sessions were the norm, especially given the possibility of clouds interfering with the necessary sunlight and of wind disturbing mane and tail hair. The vagaries of weather, not to mention the mood of photographer, trainer, and horse, made intense photo sessions a hurry-up-and-wait affair, playing peek-a-boo with the fitful sun while trying to ensure the photographer's interest, trainer's patience, groom's preparation, and horse's perfect stance. Hours of preparing and waiting would go for naught, and sometimes whole day or two-day-long visits, but then magic would strike, and the photographer would fire off a spectacular photograph or string of photographs of two, three, four, or more horses. An especially strong session would leave owner and trainer buoyed with hope until months later the package of proofs would arrive, proving or disproving their anticipation. Owners and trainers would then spend evening after evening shuffling through multiple proofs of the half-dozen to dozen horse subjects for the finest photographs to order. The photographs meant more than advertising. They were permanent records of the fleeting beauty of a precious horse.

One wouldn't suspect it, but the photography itself was one of the most perilous things that trainers and grooms did on the farm. Frankly, I'd far rather break a green horse to saddle or cart than to be the handler for the photograph of a mature stallion, for all its peril. Stallions are never more impressive in their stance than when put nose to nose with another stallion. They bow their neck, flatten their croup, flare their nostrils, and strain every muscle to impress their competitor that they are the dominant animal. One never paddocks or pastures a stallion with another stallion or even puts them in adjacent paddocks or pastures across a sturdy fence. If one did, then only one stallion would return to the barn that night. Loose stallions will attack one another with a roaring fury and force that no trainer can discourage or abate. A stallion broken loose on a farm is an instant disaster, sure to result in the stallion seeking out the stall or pen of another stallion, there to engage in equine war. Yet that very fury is what makes a photographer insist that the groom bring another stallion just a little closer, closer, closer, to see if the photography subject will swell muscles, bow neck, and flair nostrils just one bit more. The trainer then must somehow keep the photography subject perfectly posed, camera-side foreleg just ahead and camera-side rear leg well behind. Try keeping a stallion perfectly still while it prepares to kill another stallion brought nose to nose with it. Photographing mares and young horses involved other challenges for the trainer to hold the subject perfectly posed and still while grooms or assistants frightened the poor subjects with large mirrors, shaken sheet metal, plastic bottles of rock, and fire extinguishers. Trainers and helpers would need a long, quiet trail ride to calm the nerves and restore sensibility after the photographer left. But the photographs of God's most impressive animals were well worth it.

11

Feeding

Horses eat—a lot. Referring to horses, one wag once said not to own anything that eats while you sleep because that thing will eat you out of house and home. Fortunately, horses eat grain-and-hay commodities that are most of the time reasonably cheap. Yet they do eat their way through a lot of those commodities. While mom and pop may run in to pick up a sack of grain and bale of hay for the backyard horse, like going to the grocery store every week, a horse farm of any size requires substantial deliveries of both hay and grain. We would sometimes take a pickup truck or larger truck and trailer over to the grain mill or out to a hay farm to load up. Once in a while, we would even go out in the hay fields to load hay wagons with the fresh bales, getting not ony the freshest hay but also a discount on each bale for picking it up in the field. More often, trucks from the grain mill or hay farm would deliver the necessary large loads. We once had a tractor-trailer deliver from out of state an enormous flatbed of pelleted feed, some of which we then sold to local horse owners to defray the feed cost. It seemed like a good idea until raccoons squeezed into the barn's storage and tore through the paper bags. The cleanup, entailing letting the horses slowly eat their way through mounds of pelleted feed, took just a few short weeks. Horses eat—a lot.

Pellets are a modern accommodation, an effort to broaden what a horse will eat and thereby lower feed costs. Yet who knows what's in them? They look like ground-up green chaff pressed into pill-sized form. Although pellets purport to be scientifically mixed, soundly balanced, and wholly nutritious, I didn't think that our horses looked any good on them. And like humans offered health food, some horses just wouldn't eat pellets. A horse's favorite food is invariably a rich grain mix, mostly crimped or crushed oats, barley, crushed corn, and molasses sweetener. Pellets come from the factory in fifty-pound paper bags, easy to carry slung over a shoulder. Mixed grain comes from the grain mill in hundred-pound burlap sacks, a little too fat to toss over a shoulder and so instead cradled in both arms to lug around in a duck walk. Fresh-mixed grain smells heavenly. My mentor's farm used to crush its own oats to mix its own grain, the crushed-oat smell mingling deliciously with the smell of the sweet molasses. The sound of the grain cart would send the stalled horses into a fever of jumping about and whinnying. Some of them would murmur in low voices as the cart approached. A pudgy older breeding mare who needed barely a whiff of grain would make such pitiful whimpering sounds in anticipation that my wife would roll her eyes and laugh. We tried the popular remedy of putting larges stones in her grain bucket to slow down her eating, but she would still quickly suck up her little bit of grain as she banged the noisy stones frantically out of the way with her little muzzle.

For show horses preparing for a major show, we supplemented grain with various special mixes, like a pump or two of a thick orange-smelling liquid. Horses loved that stuff, diving into the pump-soaked grain. It also gave them incredible energy. After a few days of pumps, you could hear the horses bouncing off the stall walls as you went about your daily business. You had to be careful not to give them too much of it, which wasn't hard because it was incredibly expensive, obtained through the veterinarian. The feed store offered cheaper and safer supplements, like smaller red pellets scooped out of little white-plastic buckets or a yeast-like powder a tablespoon of which was said to be enough. To me, none of it but the orange-smelling pumps seemed to make much difference. But scooping out something special for the best horses made one feel like one was making a difference. We also kept mineralized salt blocks in the horse's grain buckets. Keeping a show horse at just the right weight was important to its competition success. A little too heavy, and the horse loses something of its finest features, like the narrow throatlatch. Too light, and the horse loses something of its imposing mass. Getting horse to gain or lose weight, though, is pretty easy: a little more or less of the grain scoop does it. Those doing the feeding, if not the trainer, know the trainer's wishes down to the quarter of a scoop.

Hay is an equally big deal for horses, not that they crave it like grain. Hay's big role is that a horse's digestion needs quality and quantity daily roughage. The quantity is important both to fill the horse's gut as nature intended and to occupy the horse for the couple of hours that slowly munching through the morning and evening hay requires. Horses are grazing animals. Their digestion needs bulk, and their minds need grazing-like activity. Hay supplies both. Few things are as peaceful as listening to a stable full of horses pull whisps of hay from the racks to munch, after having partially satisfied their hungry stomachs quickly consuming their grain. Hay quality is important because moldy hay can quickly give horses a deadly bout of colic. For better or worse, horses don't vomit. Whatever they eat must pass on through their stomach and intestines. Bad hay quickly leads to bad digestion, intestinal blockages, and a burst intestine. Feed bad hay in the evening, and a reactive horse, especially if unattended, may be dead by morning. We had several horses have bouts of colic, as does every trainer, given that it has other causes beyond bad feed. We also had one horse die of colic. Horse trainers are *very* particular about hay, and wisely so. One of the first things that a new farmhand learns is to check every flake of hay, meaning every four-inch-thick section of hay that peals naturally off the bale. One end of a bale may be fine while the bale's middle or other end may be moldy. Cows can eat anything, including silage. Not horses.

The wag who said not to own anything that eats while you sleep could have added not to own anything that poops while you sleep. What goes in must come out. Cleaning stalls is an unending horse-farm chore. It never stops, although one can diminish the chore somewhat by keeping horses out in the paddocks and pastures in the cool spring and fall days with reasonably warm nights. Otherwise, one is cleaning stalls constantly. If the weather gets especially bad, either in blizzard or late-summer heat, and the horses must be in stalls for most or all day and night, then the chore is best done daily, otherwise every other day. Wait three or four days, and you have a major project. In my middle teens, before I was training, I worked cleaning stalls for a breeder who just put in fresh bedding over the dirty bedding all week, leaving the once-a-week cleaning for the weekend help. Oh boy, what a disaster. I never worked so hard in a day than pitchforking stall after stall of urine-and-manure laden straw onto the tractor-pulled spreader. My brother had already started working at the farm, and so when I joined him, we worked in pairs, one on each side of the hallway of each barn, as we moved the spreader forward from stall to stall. We'd feed and water the horses starting at 7:30 a.m., start pitching manure by 8 a.m., and not stop except for an exhausted lunch break until 4:30 p.m. when it was time to feed and water the horses again.

When working that hard, the body looks for little breaks. When the spreader filled with manure, the privilege was to jump on the tractor to take the manure out to the field for spreading. A few leisurely minutes sitting on the tractor driving circles around the field was far better than lugging straw bales up and down the barn's hallway and shaking them out in the clean stalls. My brother had the spreader privilege because he was older, had started before me, and already knew the ins and outs of the farm equipment. Soon, though, he started letting me take it out now and then, for which I was deeply grateful. Yet on one of my first tries, I drove the tractor up over the crown of a hill heading into a hay field where we spread manure in winter, only to promptly mire the tractor and spreader in a snow drift. The breeder, who after a week of running his farm mostly alone tried to use his Saturday mornings for recovery and for town things, had to come out to the field to drag the spreader and tractor out of the drift backward using his old farm truck. Wow, you didn't want to make that man unhappy.

A long time passed before I got to spread manure again. Who'd think that spreading manure was a privilege? Everything is relative. I cleaned stalls without regret everywhere that I trained horses, even though as a trainer my time was better spent working and riding horses. The wear and tear of riding horses, mostly bouncing around on a sore rear and chafed knees, with tired neck, hips, arms, and shoulders, is different from the wear and tear of cleaning stalls, which is all back, leg, and shoulder muscle. Cleaning stalls was a reprieve from the bouncing around, mental concentration, and frequent frustration of riding horses, just as feeding and watering horses was a reprieve from either training or cleaning. Horse farms always offer, indeed demand, some of the same work and some different work to do. The hard work of cleaning stalls and lugging hay and straw bales had one other benefit. In high school gym class, I could effortlessly scurry up the rope to the ceiling and easily pull my bony weight up the arms-only pegboard. Because I used to run the half-mile uphill from where the school bus dropped me off after school, in time to work, feed, and water the horses, I also easily outran most boys my age. For horse trainers, fitness generally isn't a problem.

Just to make cleaning stalls a little harder, the breeder had a few horses who had to remain in the stall while we cleaned around them. The mares close to foaling were not a problem. You just shoved them out of the way when you needed to do so. Some of the skittish yearlings were harder because you had to be sure that they didn't try to dart out the stall door and into the spreader. But the hardest stalls to clean were of the stallions, especially one stallion Cocoa, an almost-black liver chestnut Morgan Horse with a neck so thick and powerful that he looked like an equine locomotive. Cocoa almost never got out of his stall into a paddock for exercise because every other horse on the farm had to be inside, or Cocoa would break through fences to go breed or kill them. Because he never got out other than when the breeder would let him dash around the indoor arena for a few minutes, Cocoa had so much pent-up energy that the slightest noise or motion would cause him to whirl about the stall. Cleaning his stall with him in it was like trying to bluff a water buffalo into letting you pick a daisy from under his belly.

Cleaning stalls at that farm, though, helped me learn and appreciate the rhythms, patterns, and efficiencies that stable work involves. Feeding and watering horses twice a day is the impregnable pattern. Whatever else one does in a day, one feeds and waters the horses twice, timely. You cannot be even a half-hour late in feeding horses without risking some protest, in the form of banging on the stalls. Watering horses at that old-school breeder's main barn was a special event because the breeder refused to keep water buckets in the stalls. Instead, he'd let each horse out of its stall to walk, trot, or canter down the barn's long hallway to a water trough at one end, where the horse could drink its fill before returning to its stall. One by one or sometimes, in the case of old mares or young fillies, two by two, the horses came down the hall to drink. If two helpers were present, then one opened the stall door to shoo the horse down to drink, while the other stood at the trough to shoo the horses back to their stalls when finished. Some horses required leading down the hall to water, especially colts or stallions that would otherwise stop and harass the other horses in their stalls. And some new horses you could lead to water but not get to drink, as the proverb warns. Those horses would surely drink the next time, if the breeder didn't relent and give them a sip from a bucket back at their stall. But most horses knew and respected the routine. The breeder explained that it gave him a chance to inspect every horse to ensure its good health.

The locomotive-like Cocoa, though, got his own special treatment. The moment you opened his door for watering, he leapt out to clatter at a strong canter down to the water trough. Better not pull the door only halfway open because he'd slam the rest of the way through anyway. You also had to watch him so that he didn't stop to bellow at another horse's stall, but a threat with the broom would get him on his way again to the trough. Once there, he wouldn't just sip with his lips like other horses or even put his muzzle well in to guzzle as some horses would do on hot days. Instead, he would dunk his head in nearly up to the eyes, so that his muzzle and nostrils were inches under water. On a hot summer day, he would occasionally put his eyes under, too. When finished, he would look briefly for some mischief until admonished sharply back toward his stall. But on his run back to his stall, he would invariably snatch up with his teeth a whole bale of hay, until then stacked neatly along the hall for feeding in the morning. He would canter down the hall with the bale in his teeth until again admonished, when he would drop the bale and leap back into his stall. Cocoa was, in short, a one-horse wrecking gang, of which his breeder owner was inestimably proud.

An inexplicable thing happened several years later, in my last year as a junior (and thus presumptively amateur, although I was already training horses for fees) rider. This old-school breeder for whom I first worked cleaning stalls, as tough a horseman as I've known, had softened, or maybe I'd just grown up. In any case, he had taken a small string of Arabian horses to the State Fair, which had been his habit. Yet to my surprise, he had also brought the locomotive but now aged Cocoa because, conveniently, at the State Fair the Arab and Morgan divisions overlapped. Cocoa, the aging breeder told me, was making his swan song, a final appearance. Years earlier, when cleaning the breeder's stalls, I hadn't realized that Cocoa had been a champion halter and Western horse. I only knew that the breeder revered the stallion and that Cocoa had a few Morgan offspring around the area. At the State Fair, the breeder for a last time showed Cocoa at halter and Western, once again doing well, probably more on laurels than merit. But then the breeder asked me to ride Cocoa in a junior-rider class. I was stunned. I hadn't worked for him for years and had never seen Cocoa ridden, no less ridden him myself. All that I could remember of Cocoa was the terror that his incredible strength, quickness, and energy had struck in me. Show-ride Cocoa, though, I did, and he turned out to be a perfectly mannerly black ball of equine fury, a gift from the old breeder to me that I had no idea he would even consider. Grace and generosity leave powerful imprints.

12

Family

Horse world is a family affair. Family farms and family training stables featured skilled fathers and mothers before too long giving way to even more-skilled sons and daughters. The nation's best-known and most-successful trainers had parents, spouses, brothers, sisters, sons, and daughters filling important roles, often as business managers, confidantes, and grooms but also training, showing, and sometimes even competing for National Championships. My mentor trainer was an example, whose wife did a great deal of the administrative work and both of whose sons followed him into the training business and were successful with their father and on their own. Another couple owned their own breeding and training farm, the husband doing most of the showing but the wife also competing and winning at the highest level. They raised four children at the shows, at first in diapers, soon grooming horses, and eventually taking over not just the bulk of the physically challenging training and showing but eventually, as they married and had their own children, the whole farm operation as their own. Another couple bred Arabian horses while managing a cattle and feed operation. Their children did all the horse training and showing, in addition to working for dad in the cattle operation.

These families were horse world's bedrock, entering every class for which they could qualify, never mind their chances of winning, and always game for another show. They won and lost together, laughed and cried together, and grew up and grew old together. They also had a lot of fun sharing the best of life together, although the fun didn't always work out exactly as planned. The family with the cattle operation, for instance, had a stalwart old show gelding that had served as the first show horse for every one of the four young children, before they moved on to showing the more-talented and challenging show horses and stallions. The old gelding was on his last child, a rough-and-tumble boy with more energy and less sense than his older siblings. The boy was showing off to his young friends how he could run up behind the old gelding, put his hands on the gelding's croup, and vault onto the gelding bareback. The boy, though, missed the gelding's twitching tail, pinned ears, tossing head, and other fair warning signs of growing intolerance. As the boy ran up from behind for the next vault, the gelding gave the boy a perfectly timed double-barreled kick right in the chest. The boy fell back unconscious, blood oozing from his mouth, his friends reasonably concluding that the boy was dead. The always-on-hand ambulance promptly removed him to the hospital. Fortunately, he was back at the show later in the day chagrined but none the worse for wear.

These up-down, down-up events were the stuff of horse-show life. No show was quite like another. The variables were too many. At one show in Central Indiana, my wife and I watched a thunderstorm roll in to knock flat the cornfields surrounding the fairgrounds, the wind tearing at the tack curtains, tables, chairs, and other fancy appointments around the barn's stalls. Wind, rain, snow, cold, or heat could all change the character of a show from pleasant recreation to pure survival. We had snow and freezing temperatures in Central Ohio on Memorial Day, floods in one location, and sweltering heat in another. Children or parents, or trainers or grooms, would suddenly take sick, changing the operation's entire delicate order. Horses would come up lame or sick, and trucks or trailers would break down. In every instance, the horse-show families would adjust as best they could, drawing on their ingenuity, resolve, and relationship. The beauty of the challenges was that no one family member could remain upset at another for long. Everyone had too much to do, too much to handle, the next chore to complete or opportunity to pursue. One seldom saw arguments, never saw fights. Despite the abundant expensive tack stored in open stalls, theft was almost unknown. Deceit had little place where all knew and had to trust and cooperate with every other. Lines blurred between families, as parents watched for the welfare of children who were not their own.

My family was not a horse family when I was growing up. My father helped my mother get two trail-riding horses when my brother was fifteen and I was thirteen. My mother and brother rode, while at first, I did not. But soon, the sport of it attracted me. My parents helped me buy from a nearby small farm a spooked young bay mare, one so untrustworthy of humans that the owners could not catch her. I spent days trying to coax the mare out of her little pasture and into the shed where I could corner her, get a halter on her, and teach her again to lead and trust humans—a good first lesson in the flight instinct of horses. I somehow gained the trust of the spooked young mare, soon broke her to saddle, which was an even more surprising feat for a young teen who hadn't a clue about horses, and then showed the mare at the 4H fair the next summer, the only show at which my brother also competed with his trail-riding horse. By age fifteen, I was riding a flighty but handsome Arabian gelding that my mother had purchased but for whom the training challenge had proved too much. By the sheer volume of classes in which the gelding and I competed together the next summer, we won the year-long high-point horse. We weren't very good, but we were getting a lot of practice together. By the following summer, my mother had taken back her now-thoroughly trained gelding, and I had graduated to Elixir, whom I trained under the watchful eye of my new mentor.

My father took no part in the care or training of the horses. As an architect and builder, his contribution was in designing and building barns and arenas, and as an amateur photographer in taking photographs of everything. I only have a couple dim recollections of my father doing anything directly with horses. At my mother's insistence, he once took us all trail riding at a stable up North, long before we owned any horses. Rented trail horses at a public riding stable are savvy to their neophyte riders. We got only a little way away from the barn before his mount turned quickly and set off for the barn at a dead run. As he flew by us yelling *whoooaaa* to no avail, I could see my father gripping the saddle horn to stay on while the reins flapped loose. Fortunately, he made it back to the barn without falling off, a significant credit to him because riding a galloping horse as it dodges other horses and ducks under tree limbs is not easy. Trail-riding-stable horses can be extremely savvy of their riders' limitations.

My one other recollection of my father working with a horse was when he once offered to exercise a young horse by lunging it in an outdoor ring behind the barn. The horse knew well how to lunge, and so I left it to him until I heard him hollering. Peeking out the back of the barn, I saw him holding a cigar in his mouth and a bottle of beer in one hand while he tried to constrain the young horse with the other hand on the lunge line. Rather than turning with the horse as it moved in circles around him, he was standing stationary and passing the lunge line over his head with each circle of the horse. I strolled out to suggest that he turn with the horse so as not to frighten it with the lunge line passing over his head, but he explained that he had gotten dizzy turning in circles with the horse. That episode ended my father's career as a trainer, although he took great interest in the show competitions and the purchase and breeding of the farm's horses.

My father's designing and building barns and arenas took on a life of its own, showing that in horse world family members can contribute in many ways. As a contemporary architect with a graduate degree from MIT, my father was not content to design and build to conventional barn and arena standards. For us, he ingeniously carved a barn, arena, observation room, and office into a hillside. We constructed the barn out of cement block without the conventional mortar, which would have taken skilled labor, instead by stacking the blocks and coating them with a stucco-like material. It worked rather well, except that horses tend to kick stall walls occasionally, whether out of annoyance or accidentally when rolling in fresh shavings. Horse stalls typically have forgiving wooden walls that don't injure kicking horses. We had a few wooden-walled stalls in an older barn to which we would move the more kick-prone horses. My father also ingeniously used a three-quarter-inch-thick cardboard-like material for the new barn's exterior, which was inexpensive but prone to easy puncture. His best innovation, though, was the translucent-plastic roof over the entire arena, allowing the sun to heat the arena in winter. Of course, the arena got so blistering hot in the summer as to be unusable on sunny days, but the tradeoff was tolerable. He and my mother sold the farm years later to an ostensible horseman who instead grew marijuana in the hothouse arena, landing in federal prison for the offense. The arena probably made a better hothouse than riding arena.

My brother, while not a horseman, managed my father's building projects for a time, including building a spectacular barn and arena for a national dressage-horse trainer. My father's building projects seemed always to present their own adventures, perhaps in part because of his creative designs. My brother was the construction manager helping add an unconventional two-story addition to our hillside barn. He and a carpenter built and raised the first huge two-story frame wall, only to see it tip over in a puff of wind and shatter down the hillside. Later, when my father and brother built the dressage trainer's huge arena, bad winter weather prevented them from setting the arena's enormous poles in the drilled ground holes, leaving the holes exposed through the winter. By early spring, the two-foot diameter holes had filled with water, sagging and spreading the neat holes into ten-foot-wide ill-defined bogs. My exasperated brother had to wade into the bogs with a shovel trying to relocate and clear the holes. Once constructed, though, the mammoth arena, more than twice the square footage of a conventional arena and with extra height up to the trusses, was stunning, especially with its translucent plastic roof brilliantly lighting the arena floor and horses, hot though it was. The dressage trainer sold the facility not long later.

My wife had a somewhat similar upbringing in horses to mine. She, too, got a horse in her early teens, around which she then focused her time and centered her ambitions. She, too, competed in 4H with a mixed-breed horse before purchasing her sweet Arab gelding and moving on to Arabian show competitions. While her father and mother encouraged and supported her horse interests, and even briefly sent her off to a horse college, they were not directly involved in the care, training, or competitions. Instead, my wife accompanied friends and other families to shows and had their help in fostering and satisfying her horse interests. My wife was a beautiful rider, possessing a poise, both physically and emotionally, that she passed on to our smart and beautiful daughter. I loved to watch my wife ride and loved working with her on her mount's performance. She was a confident English rider, but her most-elegant performances were in sidesaddle, which she rode Western. Having both one's legs on one side of the horse, one leg hitched up high over the other, is a precarious and difficult way to ride, but she made it look easy. She won sidesaddle classes on a former National Champion Western horse and would have won her own National Championship in sidesaddle if the horse had not come up lame at the annual competition.

My wife contributed to our training endeavor in innumerable other ways, including picking out the tack curtains, painting the trunks, and drawing and painting a beautiful logo. The two of us poured our energies, imagination, and creativity into our work together in times that in retrospect seem idyllic. Our best year was living in an old farmhouse rent-free across from the stables where we rented a barn wing and conducted our public-training business. Although we paid for the barn wing, we got the housing rent free in exchange for feeding the whole stable's horses on Sunday mornings. We had almost no money, just enough to make ends meet month to month, plus the value of the couple horses that we owned. But on a Saturday or Sunday afternoon, we could ride two horses a mile down a dirt road to an orchard to buy a cheap cup of fresh-pressed cider and hot donuts straight out of the fryer. Our dogs could run free all day and night. And we had miles of rolling hills over which to ride and drive the horses. Neither of us regret a minute of it, although neither of us regret moving on to more-responsible living. Every young couple should have the few years of rich, roller-coaster adventure that we had together.

13

Farms

One of the great rewards of committing one's career to horse world is the settings in which one then works. Horse farms are some of the most picturesque and idyllic places on earth. A decent farm must have pastures, paddocks, and rings, the pastures to graze horses young and old, the paddocks to turn loose the individual colts and stallions for daily outdoor exercise, and the rings in which to work the horses. The large pastures, sometimes stretching over the hills and out of sight, and the smaller paddocks, run after run of them clustered around the barn, spread horses all over the farm, near and far, some frolicking, others grazing, and others sleeping on three legs, fourth leg comfortably cocked, in the shade if hot and in the sun if not. The eye always has fresh points of interest as one surveys the pastoral scene for the location, mood, and health of the horses. The rings are where the action takes place, the focal point for riding and training. The farm may use either white-board or darker creosote-painted wood fences, in two or three rails, although my ingenious-architect father arranged to have a conveyor company cut leftover rubber belts into four-inch strips to string between wood posts and tree trunks in the fence lines. Stables do not use wire fences for horses because horses would get tangled crashing into them. More than once, we saw a horse running in our pasture bounce off the rubber fencing.

One farm on which my wife and I worked had a good-sized pond in the middle of one of its large, rolling pastures, visible from both the long, winding, asphalt driveway accessing the farm and from the working ring beside the barn. We had our dogs loose on the farm when we were there, and the dogs would meander around checking on the horses and scouting for geese, crows, or other large birds to chase for fun. When the dogs would trot out to check on the pond, the geese lining the banks would plop into the pond and paddle out a way for safety. One of the dogs, an Australian Shepherd named Sabrina, would plop into the water to swim after them or perhaps to swim with them—we were never sure because sometimes she would just swim circles rather than swim in their pursuit. Whenever she approached a goose, she would make quiet little yips with her mouth closed, which it needed to be as low in the water as she swam. Exhausted with her swim, she would climb out, shake off the water, and flop over on the grass to wiggle back and forth scratching her back.

These and a dozen other visual rewards were what one gained just walking around outdoors surveying the farm. Horse farms force one to get out and walk. The time may be early in the day or late, summer or winter, Wednesday or Sunday, but one is still outdoors walking around the farm. Horses must be led to out to pasture after a winter's night in the barn and then back to the barn before nightfall. If they are not at the pasture or paddock gate, then one must walk out to find and retrieve them, perhaps with a scoop of grain to rattle in a bucket as enticement, in which case they may come at a hungy run. Rarely, one must play tag trying to catch an unwilling horse with the illusion of cornering it, when horse and human both know that the human is no match for the size or speed of the horse. If the horses live in the pasture with a shed for shelter rather than coming in and out of stalls in the barn, then one must still walk out daily or more to check on their water, dump grain in feed bins, and in the winter chuck hay in the racks or on the shed's floor. If the summer pasture is so rich that the pastured horses need no grain or hay, and the water source is automatic or near, then one must still periodically walk out to corral the horses for breeding, farrier or veterinarian care, or sorting into other pastures. Caring for the horses keeps one constantly out and about the farm, enjoying the fresh air and vistas.

The farms also keep one hardy, when the weather makes the walks and vistas less enjoyable. We once had a series of four consecutive winter-weekend blizzards with below-zero temperatures, high winds taking the wind chill into double-digits below zero, and stinging snow.

The cold was so severe that the electric heaters in the outdoor water tubs and indoor tanks could not keep the horse water from freezing. That challenge meant carrying water to the outdoor pastures where several horses had sheds in which to shelter, to hold the water in a bucket for the horses to drink. The task may sound manageable, except remember that you can lead a horse to water but not make it drink. Just keeping the horses alive and reasonably protected took everything we had. Nothing else, like training, got done. But even severe-weather days had their own beauty on the farm. The sun, sky, frost, trees, hills, and grass take on colors, textures, and appearances that one has never imagined possible, as if the weather had suddenly transported one to another planet.

My parents' farm where my wife and I first lived and worked together was itself beautiful but surrounded by even more beautiful lands. Two adjacent farms, one separated only by our pasture fence and the other across the narrowest dirt road, kept rolling hayfields and small flocks of sheep. Farmers may disagree, but to horse lovers, hayfields are by far the prettiest lands and hay—that which horses eat—the best crop. Horses also eat oats and corn, but one cannot gallop through a corn or oat field without leaving destroyed crops. Hayfields suffer little or no insult from a galloping horse. The owners of those two sheep farms, elderly married and widowed sisters, didn't allow us regular entry, but vacant fields adjacent to their farms did have similar rolling fields in which to ride, bordered by tall woodlots. One of those rolling fields, just up the dirt road and hidden by surrounding woodlots, had a great bowl shape to it. The horses loved to gallop down into the bowl so that their momentum would carry them back up and out the bowl's other side, although we, their riders, may have enjoyed it more. The field's uncut grass would grow so tall in late summer that the horses would have to part it with their runs, leaving behind them vague trails.

The district also had several gravel pits, some of them closed. Gravel pits are probably better places for dirt bikes, all-terrain vehicles, target shooting, and other mechanical sport, but we also made them a place for our share of horse fun. Farther away, a couple of miles down dirt roads, was a vast metropolitan park that had a long lake, beach, other amenities, and miles of little-used roads and trails over rolling hills covered with open fields and dense woodlots. I proposed to my wife at that park after a long bicycle ride to an overlook over the beach. I can't recall why we didn't ride horses, as we had on other occasions, but it was probably to do something unique. We didn't ride bikes around the farm. We rode or, on occasion drove a horse with the two-wheeled buggy. I recall driving a mare that needed a good workout the three or so miles to a Dairy Queen on the other side of the park. Imagine proposing a trail ride or buggy ride to your wife or friend and having all those choices of pursuits and directions. And it wasn't just the freedom of heading off in any direction on horseback. The fun was in the talk, sights, and escapades along the way.

The productive end of a horse farm is horses, not hay, grain, cattle, or sheep. Horse farms thus mean breeding, which is a world unto itself. Owners and trainers like the product of breeding—the exciting new fillies and colts, filled with promise. But I didn't meet any owner or trainer who liked breeding itself. Uncertainty colors the whole affair. One must first ascertain whether the mare is at that three-to-four-day point in her monthly cycle when she can conceive. The mare's willingness to entertain breeding usually determines whether her cycle is at the right point, although not always. Handlers determine the mare's willingness to entertain breeding by *teasing* the mare (yes, that's what they call it) with a stallion. Some stallions make better teasers than others. A good teaser takes a strong but manageable interest in the mare. A bad teaser takes too little interest or, conversely, too strong and unmanageable of an interest. One is no better than the other. One needs just the right amount of noise and nuzzling to determine the mare's interest. And just because a stallion is a good teaser doesn't mean that the stallion gets to breed any mares. Mare owners choose stallions for their conformation, performance talent, and color, not for their amorous skill.

After the noise and racket of teasing all the farm's mares that are currently scheduled for breeding, usually done every other day to ensure accurate charting, one has the necessary short list of breeding candidates. For popular stallions, the list may be more than one mare, in which case one must plan for artificial insemination of all candidates. Sparing the details, either way, artificial or natural, the process means a lot of washing to prevent infections, and more noise and racket. Handlers routinely twitch mares, meaning to twist a short rope around their upper lip, for greater control and to ensure the stallion's safety. Handlers also routinely use a chain around the stallion's nose or under the upper lip, for greater control and to ensure the mare's safety. Despite the precautions, if a trainer, handler, or veterinarian is going to get hurt, then the injury is most likely to happen during breeding. The farm learns the results of the whole effort a month later when the mare is or is not interested in breeding. A veterinarian can rectally palpate the mare a little while later to confirm the pregnancy. Some mares go a whole four-month breeding season getting bred but not conceiving. Owners and breeders value stallions and mares in part by their conception rates, suggesting again the level of uncertainty and likelihood of frustration. Breeding horses is for the patient person.

Breeding also means foaling. A mare's gestation period is eleven months, meaning in theory that a mare can have a foal every spring, which some do. The Arabian registry follows a calendar year. Owners thus try to time the foaling for early in the year, January if possible, so that their foals have grown to the greatest size possible for the next fall's weanling futurity. A January or February foal has a big advantage over a March or April foal, the latter of which may not even compete in the fall futurity. Foaling is thus a winter and early spring affair. Although operations vary, trainers are usually responsible for breeding and foaling, just as they are for most everything else on the farm. Although video cameras long ago made a difference, my wife and I spent many nights getting up in the middle of the night to check on mares and a few more nights sleeping in the barn in midwinter hoping to catch a mare who the day before looked as if she might be ready to foal. Signs of delivery are a little different but about as predictable as they are for pregnant women, except that the mare can't tell you how or what she is feeling. Mares invariably foal at night, though, and usually in the middle of the night or before dawn in the very early morning. The sounds of a barn at night are different than daytime sounds. The grain and hay are all soon eaten, diurnal munching giving way to nocturnal murmurs, shifts, and signs of digestion. Mares pace and lay down and get up and lay down again when about to foal, easy to sense even when in a light sleep.

Why should a breeder be present for foaling? If the undelivered foal's position is incorrect or compromised, such as for a breech delivery, then a veterinarian would be necessary, in which case the urgent call goes out. But short of something so rare and serious, the mare will likely deliver with little or no assistance. One hazard for which a breeder watches and can help is when the mare lays down against a wall. Mares generally foal in a stall rather than pasture so that mare and foal are secure and the breeder can be near to help. Stalls, though, are small for a mare on her side straining to deliver a foal. Breeders often have a double stall for delivering mares, giving greater room. But still, a mare will lay down tight against a wall on occasion, when a breeder can help by urging the mare to move or moving the foal from against the wall as the mare strains it out. The greater help, though, is with the foal itself. The placenta covers the foal's nostrils during delivery until the foal's forelegs tear it aside. Uncovering the nostrils so that the foal does not suffocate, tangled up in the placenta, is a routine and critical first step.

Once the mare delivers the foal and placenta and rises again to her feet, the bigger challenge begins. Mares delivering their first foal are not always so sure what just happened, or so it can seem. Mares have kicked or otherwise treated too roughly, and thereby killed, their newborn offspring. I recall a young Egyptian mare doing so at my mentor's farm when I was there, after we had struggled to introduce mare to foal. Some restraint of the anxious mare as she paces about the stall so that she does not step on or otherwise injure the foal is often appropriate. The foal needs its own help. Drying it with some straw or a towel to stop its shivering can help. More significantly, within a half hour to hour, the foal should have gotten to its feet, a rather incredible accomplishment considering its tiny frame, head, and neck, absent muscle, but ridiculously long legs. The foal's flopping and stumbling about in valiant, humorous, and touching efforts to rise inevitably leads to the foal crashing into the stall's walls, unless the breeder is present to cradle the foal in the breeder's arms. You want to do something instantly meaningful and unforgettable? Help a foal take its first critical steps.

Yet then the real challenge begins, which is to get the foal to nurse within the first couple or few hours. The mares, especially those just having had their firstborn, are not always so willing to stand still for the awkward foal to nose and bump blindly about while searching for the mare's tender milk teats. For its part, the still-teetering foal has no clear idea what it is trying to do, only some instinctual appetite and urge it has never yet attempted to fill. The foal soon makes suckling gestures with its lips with no idea of the moving target of its satisfaction. Harder yet, to nurse requires the foal to stretch its neck out and its head up, better with a twist of the neck left or right to reach the teat up between the mare's hind legs. God had a good sense of humor when designing this novel arrangement. Breeders may take patient hours putting drops of mare's milk on their fingertips while trying to guide the foal's suckling lips toward their hidden goal. A prolonged process tires the foal, adding to the urgency of making the critical connection. Somehow, the process usually works out to the breeder's great relief and greater relief of the mare and foal. Rarely, the foal is too weak to nurse or the mare rejects the foal, which means nursing the foal from a bottle, both an incredibly laborious months-long chore and one that inevitably leaves the foal weakened and even stunted.

Nursing mares are a farm's pride and joy. Within a few days of foaling, mare and foal can join other nursing mares in paddocks or pastures. A pasture of several nursing mares each with its foal by its side or nearby is a precious sight, especially when the foals gambol about playfully with one another, which they quickly begin to do. The breeder's excitement grows as foals begin to show features, like long, high-set necks, laid-back shoulders, flat croups, and fine-shaped heads, that the foals may bear when mature, although early looks can be deceiving. Four to five months later, the breeder will wean the foals, a traumatic process for foals made only slightly less so by pairing foals together. Misery loves company. The two just-weaned foals will spend a few days together in a stall where they cannot crash into and through fences trying to reach their mother. Although they are perfectly safe and well fed, by that time eating grain and hay, drinking water, and not needing their mother's milk, and their handlers make over them with all the care that one wants to give a lost child, they nonetheless look and sound pathetic, so much so that the appearance, which passes within a week or two, amuses. Soon the foals are all together in paddock or pasture, their own tribe. The mares vary in their reactions to weaning. Some look relieved, others at some loss, one supposes like when parents drop off their children at college. By the time the mares' milk dries within the next few days, though, they are over it. Young horses always launch. Their equine parents have no basement.

The small herds of five, eight, ten, or twelve late-year weanling fillies and colts make the farm the delight that it is. Weaned from their dams and without any other mature horse in their paddock or pasture, they cast about among themselves for new leadership, until volunteers step forward or take the mantle by default. Horses in herds always have a pecking order. The dominant mare is the first to get any privilege, especially the grain that the farmhand delivers into buckets at the pasture fence or flakes of hay tossed over the fence onto the ground, and will ensure so with a swift bite or kick for any challenger or pretender. The second-in-command will do likewise for the next-lower mare and so on right down through the entire pecking order. One must spread the grain and hay at sufficient intervals to ensure that each mare gets a share. Weanlings by contrast tend to huddle up at first, without social structure. But soon the hierarchy emerges, as the weanlings first chase one another about in gay play but gradually turn that play to establishing serious rank and order. As the weanlings mature through the fall and turn to yearlings in winter, the breeder must separate fillies from more-aggressive colts, who start to feel their proverbial oats. Hormones in horses work much like they do in teenagers. Bands of colts may stay together through their yearling year but grow increasingly rambunctious and destructive until their separation one by one becomes necessary.

Unless a breeder decides to pick out and show an especially impressive candidate, weanlings and yearlings get nothing but loving care. A breeder will teach the weanling to take a halter and follow a lead line, a process that tends to entail the weanlings flopping about like fish. A halter and lead, though, are necessary for the shots, hoof trimming, brushing, and other care and inspection that young horses require. In general, less handling or at least less pampering is better for the young horses' physical development, as Thoroughbred breeders prove in letting their yearlings run free in large rolling pastures. Catching and restraining wild-like yearlings for shots and hoof trimming is not a farmhand's favorite chore. Days handling yearlings are good ones to wear thick boots against getting one's toes mashed by stamping hooves. Having a mature horse step on one's foot is painful, a sure sign of the horse's disrespect for its handler. Every trainer knows that an amateur's horse will step all over one until it learns that necessary respect. But having a weanling or yearling stomp on one's toes is worse, with the full weight concentrated in the tiny hoof. Thankfully, though, yearlings soon turn into two year olds, when breeders breathe a sigh of relief as the young horse develops a modicum of sense and approaches the age of training and breeding.

Young Arabian horses generally linger around their breeder's farm until late in their second year or early in their third year. Thoroughbreds may race late in their two-year-old years and so would be off to the trainer in mid-summer. Arabians are slower to mature physically and mentally. (Some would say that they never mature mentally, with which at times one finds it hard to disagree.) Bones must close in the knee before the horse can safely carry a rider's weight. Arab trainers, though, may drive a two year old late in the year, accustoming it to bit and bridle. By age three, an Arabian is not only ready for riding but also for breeding if the owner prefers. The farm will have culled and sold late two year olds or early three year olds, preparing for the next generation. Farms thus have a natural rhythm not only day to day and season to season but also year to year. The rhythms stay the same while the horses turn over and change, lending the farm its intoxicating mix of nostalgia, hope, and freshness.

14

Shows

Horse shows are a traveling road show, a community of people repeatedly parting and coming together, with people and horses drifting in and out of the wider circle of participants the inner circle of which changes little. The participants are technically competitors but in substance more like co-workers and co-celebrants in a grand equine fellowship. The shows have a little of the feel of a popular truck stop, at once both entirely transient and yet intensely communal. The communal part develops over time but is unavoidable. One cannot see horse-show children grow up, marry, and have their own horse-show children, or horse-show couples uncouple and remarry into other horse-show couples, without gaining an increasingly strong sense of community. One comes to know not only each other's skills, ambition, and outward character but also one another's faults, foibles, eccentricities, and stark limitations. The locations change from weekend to weekend, but even the locations and their charms, conveniences, and peculiarities become familiar from season to season.

Show grounds for in-state competitions are typically modest, often old and out-of-the-way county fairgrounds. For trainers, grooms, and horses, the nice thing about county fairgrounds is that they usually have decent barns and rings designed for horses, plus plenty of open fields in which to ride, lunge, and walk the horses, park vans, and set up campers and tents. While the glamor of winning competitions at premier urban facilities may be nice, a trainer's fondest show memories are from the county fairgrounds. Fairground dining and restroom amenities may be modest, bad, or even non-existent. Our grooms and I had our share of freezing-cold showers in ancient concrete facilities (I'm hoping that I didn't put my wife through that—we often had a suitable camper or hotel). But then again, if the show occurs during the county fair itself rather than as a stand-alone event, the food at least may be quite special. Try fried chicken or roast beef and mashed potatoes cooked by the Daughters of the American Revolution, not to mention the midway's elephant ears.

State championships, regional championships, and National Championships are instead at state fairgrounds or regional convention centers, where the trainer and groom amenities can be quite decent but the setup for horses less so. I recall showering in a decent visitor's locker room at a major university's football stadium adjacent to the state fairgrounds in Louisville. The food at state fairgrounds and urban convention centers can also be decent, at least cafeterias serving hot meals and sometimes better like reliable national restaurant chains. Food on the premises becomes critical as show tasks mount and time runs short. Who has time to pile trainer and grooms into a distant-parked vehicle, navigate out of the convention-center grounds, and locate decent reasonably priced food somewhere in the city? At major shows, you won't see trainers gathering grooms for a good meal until maybe midnight, when the nearest sleepy diner's tables fill with hungry grooms stuffing themselves with missed calories. Toronto's massive convention center, where we showed at the Canadian National Championships, was another example of attractive amenities. Yet the cement floor and twenty-four-hour cold lights of a massive convention-center hall, filled with hundreds of increasingly stinky stalls and unhappy horses, can be a deafening and deadening place to care for a string of show horses for several days at once. One pines for the green grass and fresh air of a county fairground.

Easily the most spectacular show grounds at which we showed was the Horse Park at Lexington. The grand barn in which we stabled the featured stallions was spectacular, a showpiece. The rings had perfect footing, immaculately groomed. Attractive white tents shielded owners, spectators, and weary trainers and grooms from the hot sun. One could eat well on the grounds from varied concessions designed for discriminating tourists. The Horse Park also had fun and fascinating permanent exhibits to visit, leaving no need to entertain the grooms. Just being at the Horse Park was its own education and reward. But best of all, the Park is in prime rolling Kentucky-bluegrass lands. Every vista, whether at a misty daybreak, blue-sky noon, or red sunset, was worthy of a postcard. Showing at the Horse Park was a trainer's dream, even if the horses only semi-cooperated. Another favorite was the show grounds in Scottsdale outside Phoenix, for the dry air, brilliant sun, and nearby mountains and tourist attractions.

Shows have an odd sort of exhilarating and draining intensity. Each class in which one competes carries its own excitement, whether for the possibility of winning, the probability of disappointing a proud and expectant owner, or simply surviving the adventure with reputation intact. The first time in the ring with a new horse tells a trainer a lot. A horse can be a model citizen in the practice ring at home but a wreck at a show given the many horses in the show ring at once, the unfamiliar ring environs, and a show's many other distractions. Getting a green performance horse *used to the ring*, meaning familiar with the show ring's peculiar dirt, gates, railings, lights, shadows, and centerpiece (stage, speakers, flowers, shrubbery, cones) is a high priority on arrival. Otherwise, a trainer might not make it into the ring or around the ring without the threat of unseating or other embarrassment. Yet training of that type can be nearly an afterthought to the extensive unloading, setup, cleanup, grooming, registration, client support, and general management of show affairs. A show is a logistical nightmare until the team of trainer, family, grooms, clients, and horses have rehearsed and mastered their respective roles and duties.

Getting sleep at a show is a small miracle. When I began training and showing, evening classes often went late until 10 or 11 p.m., after which a few trainers or amateurs would take a quick stab at working a green horse in the ring before retiring for the night. Soon, though, trainers found that they could school several horses in the show ring at their leisure and with a degree of confidentiality if they convened their session after midnight, which basically meant working through the night while still showing during the day. Some trainers may have adjusted, like doctors or nurses who consistently work thirty-six hour shifts. I never did adjust, instead feeling miserable the next day, which seemed to me to cancel out most of the small gain from the extra work in the middle of the night. You could see some pretty interesting sessions, though, in the middle of the night, as trainers worked horses that were not ready for the performance show ring. Young trainers soon realized that the middle-of-the-night sessions, especially at National Championships or other major shows, were their own training grounds, where they could go to school simply by observing the training masters at work that those masters had hoped they could keep confidential. The sessions soon became cat-and-mouse games, trainers waiting until the gawkers had given up and gone to bed, leaving tantalizing rumors the next morning about the incredible things the weak had missed.

You can see that for the trainer and grooms, and even the owners, what goes on in the ring is only a small part of a show. Yes, show results are important. Yet what goes on outside the ring takes a great deal more time and energy than the competition itself, has a great impact on the competition, and can have a greater impact on the stable's future than what goes on in the ring. The life of the show is really back at the barns around the stable's stalls. The significance to the trainer's business of owners and prospective owners gathering with trainers back around the training stable's stalls makes stall location a big deal for horse shows. The best stalls are prominent, convenient, and sound, with features like wide aisles and sight lines to and from the show ring and other high-traffic areas. Better to be seen than out of sight. A stable is much more visible at a prominent barn's near end with lots of open gathering room for owners and prospective clients to stand around. The worst locations are out of sight, around back of temporary tents or distant barns, perhaps too near the parking lot, washrack, or manure pile. Trainers compete to befriend show and barn managers for the benefit of stall locations.

The same things that make stall location significant also make significant their decoration. Tack curtains can be a new training stable's first significant expenditure. The thick-fabric, colorful curtains enshroud the tack stall, stalls with stallions so that they cannot see and roar after other horses, and any other stalls of horses that the trainer wants to hide or protect. Thus, a training stable's colors bedeck the six, eight, ten, or twelve stalls that the stable rents at a show, giving the stable an impressive presence. Banners run along the top of the tack curtains, increasing their identity and gaiety. When trainers and grooms arrive at a show, the first task after unloading the horses, tack, and gear, and cleaning and parking the trailer, is to get the tack curtains up, stretched impressively tight and stapled to furring strips (wood lathe) brought for the purpose. Grooms and trainers get very good at quickly nailing or wiring the furring strips to wood, steel, and chain-link stalls. Carpet or dried-grass mats, rugs, deck chairs, coffee tables, lamps, coolers, and drinks quickly placed out soon make the itinerant stable seem like home away from home for owners, trainers, and grooms who will spend hours and days hanging around the stable, making friends, deals, and plans.

Despite that much of the action is back around the stables, owners especially like to sit in the grandstand with family and friends, near other owners, to watch one another's horses compete. A horse show's grandstand community is a bit like the grandstands at middle school and high school sporting events, where parents of the competing students sit to watch their kids while chatting with friends. Indeed, horse owners may have children competing in the show ring. Owners will sit a few rows up, close enough to the action to call out encouragement to their horse and its child or trainer rider or handler but high enough up for a good view of the whole ring to see if their beloved horse shines or stumbles. Owners are their own horse's cheering section, recruiting family, friends, and grooms to their clamorous cause, raining down whoops and whistles of real or feigned appreciation. Their horse's performance may genuinely excite them, or they may whoop and whistle anyway as their horse passes before the judge but then promptly turn aside to a friend to bemoan the lackluster performance. A performance class ends with the announcer calling the contestants to line up in the ring's center, following which the judge walks the line marking the scorecard to hand to the ringmaster to run to the announcer. Whoops and whistles follow announcement of winners.

Regular classes award ribbons from first through sixth or, at a bigger show, first through eighth. First-place ribbons are, of course, blue, and at a larger show may garner a stainless plate or other accompanying medallion or trophy. Second place receives a red ribbon, third yellow, fourth green, fifth white, sixth pink, and seventh and eighth no one cares and I don't remember. Championship performance classes at or near the end of the show, for each of park, English, Western, driving, combination, and other types of classes, gather winners from various divisions including stallion, mare, gelding, junior horse, and amateur rider. Championship classes award the same order of ribbons but identify the first-place winner as champion and second-place winner as reserve champion, giving out fancy tri-color ribbons with a larger stainless plate or standing trophy. Training stables collect and display the ribbons and plates or trophies prominently back at the barn, as the best form of immediate advertising. By the middle of a show, one can readily tell which trainers are having good or bad shows. Owners, though, take the ribbons and plates or trophies home. Those who pay the bills receive the spoils.

Surprisingly, trainers and grooms don't watch a lot of classes. Trainers are usually either in the ring competing or somewhere else getting work done. For their part, grooms will follow their trainer up to the ring, sticking very close to attend to any need for last-minute grooming, equipment fixes, and the like. For a park or halter class, where the horses should enter with maximum animation, grooms may even snap towels, bang on railings, and hoot and holler as their horse charge enters the ring. Grooms then need to get back to the barn to prepare the next horse or accomplish other work. If trainers or grooms do watch a class, then they tend to watch classes from the ring's railing where they can move about and more-closely observe, encourage, or caution other competitors, and chat with other grooms and trainers. Often, the action just outside the ring, involving who watches, walks and talks with, or avoids whom, entertains more than the competition in the ring. One trainer I knew, though, was such a committed loner, that he generally eschewed both standing at the rail or sitting in the lower reaches of the grandstand with or near the owners. He would climb the many steps to the highest and darkest reaches of the grandstand to sit alone, peering over the whole affair far below him, reading a newspaper, or snoozing. I tried it a few times, and the solitude and brief respite in the middle of a frantic show were heaven, but important things weren't getting done.

Trainers and grooms hanging around the ring's gate serve another purpose. Things don't always go so well in the ring. Riders fall off, equipment breaks, horses balk, and horses come up lame, each an occasion for swift groom or trainer action. Halter horses get loose in the ring when a handler drops the lead or the horse gets its leg over the lead or just runs off violently enough to free itself. A halter horse running loose in the ring can wreak havoc as it crashes into and weaves in and out of handlers and horses. The havoc increases several fold when the loose horse is a colt or stallion. Colts and stallions bellow, threaten, and kick at one another, endangering one another and handlers. A loose mare may just stand there. A loose filly may just jog and prance around for a pretty little frisk. Indeed, ringmasters have justly accused trainers of deliberately setting a beautiful young filly loose for it to parade around with its tail over its back. By contrast, a loose colt or stallion will promptly look for its best victim. Trainers don't purposely turn their stallions or older colts loose just to show off. One acute problem of one loose stallion among ten, twenty, or thirty, is that all other stallions promptly perceive the threat and opportunity, growing nearly as animated as their loose tormentor. Another acute problem is that the handler of one stallion can hardly catch the approaching loose stallion because to do so would simply bring the two stallions nose to nose. The free handler who lost the stallion must catch it, or grooms and trainers who flood the ring to help must catch it, which would be a small mark of pride, most evident when handing the stallion back to the negligent handler.

Buggy wrecks are another good reason for trainers and grooms to hang around the ring's gate, in case of need for swift emergency action. Few other spectacles mix such horror with such intrigue. The primary intrigue involves whether the driver, ringmaster, or other trainers and grooms who at the moment of the wreck were lingering about the ring are able to catch the horse before it drags its driverless buggy into other horses or buggies, causing a multi-buggy wreck. A wreck usually begins when a driver falls out of the buggy because of the buggy's sudden tip or jolt. The driver only perches on a little raised cushion in the four-wheeled formal buggy, which certainly has no seatbelts, making it surprisingly easy for the driver to tumble out. Wrecks also unfold extremely quickly. A driverless horse pulling a wide and long four-wheeled cart only needs a few more steps before hooking wheels with another cart or a post or railing, frightening the loose horse into a jump or bolt. The horror is that the loose horse inevitably ends up destroying its own buggy, leaving it running with the buggy shafts still strapped to its sides by the harness. Those broken shafts act like spears for anything with which the loose horse collides, like people and other horses. The buggy parts, driving lines, and harness lines that the loose horse drags serve to whip and further scare the loose horse into desperate flight. The other drivers know that the survival strategy is to pull quickly into the ring's center in hopes that the loose horse will simply race around and around the circle of the ring. As soon as they reach the ring's center, the other drivers will leap out of their buggies and try to unhook their own horse so that it does not become a second loose horse rampaging around the ring in the emerging catastrophe. Single-buggy wrecks happen every season, several of them. A major wreck involving multiple buggies may happen only once a season, but when it does, it can leave drivers, grooms, ringmasters, and even judges injured, horses wounded or worse, and buggy parts spread all across the ring. It definitely puts a damper on the weekend. As beautiful as a formal-driving event is, whoever first thought driving Arabian horses was a good idea and promoted show driving competition should have to watch a wreck.

Yet the intrigue of a buggy wreck is only in part who will catch the loose horse and when, before it causes what destruction. The other intrigue is which horses, drivers, and buggies are able to escape out the ring's gate while the horse runs loose. Emptying the ring of other contestants with their frightened horses and drivers, and fragile and expensive buggies, sounds like a good idea. The reason that it is not is that opening the ring's gate to allow one competitor to escape unscathed risks opening the gate to the loose horse, for it to create exponentially more hazard outside the ring. I've seen it happen, twice. A loose horse dragging parts of a destroyed buggy once forced its way out past a competitor who was trying to slip the competitor's own horse and buggy out the gate. The loose horse's escape destroyed the other buggy, but that was only the beginning of the carnage. The loose horse then made a dead run down the show's main thoroughfare, still dragging buggy pieces, scattering horses, riders, and bystanders, and endangering children, trailers, and cars. The horse disappeared into and through the parking lot filled with trucks and trailers, beyond which lay a major city thoroughfare. I don't recall whether the horse survived, but it may well not have.

The other buggy wreck in which a loose horse escaped the ring still dragging destroyed buggy parts did not escape the ring because of a competitor's fault. Ringmasters know that the loose horse must remain in the ring at all costs, no matter what the horse destroys there. They know that the greater risk involves the horse getting loose beyond the ring. Ringmasters are thus loathe to open the gate for escaping competitors, lest the loose horse also escape. In this second instance, the ringmaster wisely kept the gate firmly closed. The loose horse, though, had other ideas, taking a spectacular leap over the gate, still dragging buggy parts with it. The horse wasn't a jumper and so didn't nearly clear the gate, which meant that the horse instead did a somersault over it, the gate knocking its legs out from under it. Somehow, before trainers and grooms could leap on the horse and hold it down to extricate it from the harness and attached buggy pieces, the horse scrambled up from the slippery cement arena chute and tried to make its way down the chute and out to the daylight freedom its instincts perceived. Horses retain strong flight instincts. Fortunately, grooms and trainers converged on and restrained the horse just as it tried to resume its bolt. The horse even survived the debacle, although taking weeks to heal. So, interested in trying Arabian show-horse driving?

The saddest part of a show is packing up. Almost no matter how poorly a show starts and goes for a trainer, if classes remain in which to compete, then the show must go on. Shows do so with clear purpose (the competition) and thus imbued with reliable life and energy. Win or lose, that purpose disappears at show's end, causing the life and energy to quickly dissipate. One can have the best possible show, winning multiple championships, yet when time comes to pack up, all seems lost. The ribbons, plates, and trophies pale in comparison to the show's lost life and a trainer's lost fellowship. Yes, the thought of returning to one's home stable brings with it some comfort and great anticipation of needed rest. But the thought also reminds the trainer of the isolated hours training at home where no one sees and appreciates even the greatest possible performance. As the first trailers begin to leave the show, the emptying show grounds take on a cold feel. As the last trailers pull out, the show grounds are once again a ghost town. A few times, we stayed on at a show grounds for a day or two after the show ended before heading straight to the next show. Doing so was always a mistake, like lingering at the funeral home after the procession had already left for the interment. Far better to go straight on to the next show grounds, where anticipation would already be building for the next event. Yes, the show must go on.

15

Judges

Judges have a peculiar effect on shows and trainers. On one hand, judges mean a lot. They alone determine winners and losers. Owners and trainers succeed or fail in their designs and efforts depending on whether a judge says so. Judges also have an effect, though, on the show itself, independent of the success or failure of individual winners and losers. An efficient judge who knows how to keep a show on time, pick deserved winners, respect earnest losers, and allow the event the grandeur it deserves, makes a show what it should be. That judge makes the show worthwhile for its sound purpose in promoting good breeding, training, and performance, meaningful for competitors who can judge their progress, and intrinsically valuable as a display of social, cultural, material, and spiritual flourishing, even when one loses. A judge who lets the show fall way behind, judges haphazardly and unfairly, plays favorites, and disrespects those who lose but should win or those who lose and should lose, deprives the show not only of its purpose but of its magnificence. The horses will always be impressive creatures, but their splendor grows when properly staged in sound and celebratory competition.

One finds hard telling how judges acquire the skill to judge well. Great judges seem born more than made. They tend not to be breeders or trainers, or at least not prominently so, because of the conflicts that both judging and breeding or training would instantly engender. Either that, or they are breeders or trainers from a distant part of the country, so that they do not judge horses they bred, trained, or compete against. No matter their experience, as breeders, trainers, or neither, judges must know not only what a horse should be and trainer should do but also what the event should itself represent. Those gifts seem more natural than learned. Great judges seem to come from great horse families or traditions, perhaps having just crossed over from a life in another breed to embrace judging your breed, with true appreciation but no history or conflicts. Yet over time, one can also see judges grow in the role. Judges may start at a B- or C-level circuit rather than A-level, comprised of the tiny one- and two-day local shows that don't even count toward state awards or National Championship qualification. There, with the stakes lower, new judges make every mistake that judges shouldn't make. They also see lots of poorly conformed and poorly trained horses handled and ridden by green and below-average owners and trainers. In time, they learn class management and show management and, with it, learn horse and handler evaluation.

Show managers and their committees hire judges. The choice has consequences because trainers tend to know the judges before whom they typically do well or not so well. A single judge may judge two, three, or more shows around the country or region each year at which the same trainer will appear. A trainer may thus tell in advance pretty well how the trainer and specific horses will do or not do at a certain show. For a time, I had a judge before whom one of my horses and I could hardly lose, little matter the event and quality of performance, even to the point of some embarrassment. Yet for that time, why *not* attend those shows?! Oddly, much later, I could hardly seem to win in front of that judge, no matter the event, horse, or quality of performance, to the point of great frustration. Why attend *those* shows?! In short, trainers pick shows based in part on the judges. Smaller shows have a single judge, while biggers shows may have two or three judges who divide rather than share the duties. National Championships have several judges who judge in rotating teams of three, canceling out some of the uncertainty and potential bias. When a very fine horse and rider from California just barely beat Elixir and me for a National Championship, the three judges put her first, first, and third, and me first, second, and second, her two firsts breaking the five-point tie between us. Close, but no cigar.

While all judges should judge to breed and performance standards, and most presumably try earnestly to do so without bias, judges are human. Despite standards for everything, we all like some things our way more so than another's way, whether the choice has to do with pizza, ice cream, or friends, or horses or trainers. Judges can like specific riders, handlers, or horses, or they can like certain types of riding, handling, horse, or performance. For example, some Arabian judges once liked Raffles-bred horses. Raffles was a stallion that famous early American breeder of Arabians Roger Selby imported in 1926 from Lady Crabbet's Wentworth Stud in England. Raffles was certainly an important Arabian sire in America, for many easily the most-significant of that era. His fine head, straight legs, long neck, and other sound features made him so, notwithstanding a rounder rather than properly flat croup and a dapple-grey color that some found less striking than darker bays and chestnuts. Whether by inbreeding of his strain or for other reasons, his line in later times grew to be associated with significantly smaller, less-athletic horses of that still-disappointingly rounder croup and dirty-grey color. Yet Raffles-leaning judges would nonetheless pick those little buggers out of a crowd of obviously superior horses.

Every bias works both ways. Other judges came to favor offspring and descendants of more-recent imports of Arabian horses from Poland, especially the fabulously successful Bask. Bask horses, like Raffles and other early English Wentworth-bred horses, also tend toward long necks and straight legs, but unlike descendants of the early English imports, Bask horses tend to be bay rather than grey or chestnut and tend toward powerful athleticism from a significantly more-developed hindquarter, even if they less often have the fine-featured heads of those early English imports. Some judges for a time rewarded anything that looked at all Polish, while the Raffles-looking horses couldn't get a whiff of respect. The biases, like any bias, were unfortunate in that for every typical attribute of either line of Arabian, an exception existed. My large, dark, and athletic horse Elixir, with a relatively plain-featured head, was registered as having come entirely from Wentworth-bred lines including significant Raffles influence, which should have produced exactly the opposite of his appearance. Rumors abounded that Elixir's controversial breeder had taken Elixir's dam down the road to a huge, dark, and extremely athletic Saddlebred, making Elixir a, well, bastard. The funny thing was that Elixir's dam soon produced another big chestnut offspring just like Elixir, suggesting that either the sketchy breeder did the dastardly deed twice rather than just once or, to the contrary, was entirely honest in his breeding and registration. I just trained and showed the horse.

Owners do try to influence judges with their wild cheering. Yet judges seemed to me to be largely impervious to each owner and their recruited family members and friends cheering for their own horse each time that the judge observed it, although owners surely didn't think so, given their insistence on the exhortatory practice. In a halter class, each horse approaches the judge one at a time to stand in the ring's middle while the judge circles and inspects it, before the judge watches it trot off. When the judge then turns to the next horse the next handler has set up at prideful attention along the rail, that horse's owner and friends instantly break out in rowdy throng. The clamor subsides as the handler walks the horse to meet the judge at ring center but then rises again as the handler sets up the horse for its preening maneuvers (head high, neck stretched to greatest length, muscles taut, frame tipping forward and back). Owner and friends save their greatest cheers and whistles, though, for the moment that the handler trots the horse gallantly off, hoping for an especially animated last-glimpse impression. These predictable cheers rise and fall repeatedly as the morning's halter classes wear on, contributing in their own way to the show's sense of self-importance.

For the trainer, standing a winning horse up in center ring before a prominent judge at a premier event before a raucous crowd recruited over months of show winning to the horse's championship pursuit is a satisfyingly intense experience. The trainer's first task is to get the horse's legs posed perfectly, neck arching high, ears alert, head tipping slightly toward the judge, and nostrils flaring. Better, too, if the horse rocks slightly back and forth, tracking each of the trainer's movements. Yet somewhere in that tense mix, the trainer should subtly greet the judge, especially if the judge and trainer know one another from prior competitions or outside circumstances. They may even be former mentor and apprentice, even current friends. Awkwardly, I showed once in front of my trainer mentor, at a local show where I regularly competed and where he shouldn't have been judging, given his too many other similar conflicts. I recall him judging my performances harshly, which felt appropriate. In any case, judges properly isolate themselves from competitors at show competitions. Propriety's appearance being important, one doesn't chat with the judge at the rail or restaurant. At a show, trainers generally meet the judge in the ring and only in the ring. So, a nod at last approach, eyes meeting for less than a second, and a greeting spoken out of the side of the mouth while setting the horse up, is more appropriate. Some judges are more talkative, uttering muttered wisecracks solely for the trainer friend's confidential consumption, the trainer held to stifle a smile but have a wisecrack reply to mutter when the judge comes back around the standing horse. Aren't these sorts of shared but stifled understandings the stuff of professional life?

For their part, suspicious owners keep close watch on judges for various shenanigans. Performance horses parade around and around the ring, often at considerable pace. Judges must either stand at one place in ring center facing the rail to watch each competitor fly by or step back deep toward a corner end of the ring to survey and follow the whole spinning spectacle. Judges typically hold a card on which they fleetingly write the numbers pinned to the back of the riders' suits, as the horses fly by or whenever they see something of interest. Owners, of course, wonder what the judge is writing immediately after seeing the owner's mount. If their horse has just broken gait, taken a wrong lead, dodged a shadow, pinned its ears at a passing competitor, or committed an equivalent sin, then the owner knows that the judge has just written off the owner's horse. At that point, a low ribbon or getting shut out will only disappoint, not surprise, the owner. Yet if the judge writes the owner's horse's number after a routine pass or an especially strong pass, then the owner prepares to rejoice at a win, show, or place, and will be both surprised and aggrieved, and maybe also suspicious of a conspiracy, at instead getting shut out.

Other suspected shenanigans arise due to owners and trainers naturally wanting the judge watching *their* horse at *only the best moments* and *not when the horse makes one tiny bobble*. Life doesn't work out that way, unless the judge wants it to do so. Perceptive judges can tell when a good horse is about to make a bad bobble, for instance when it approaches a misbehaving competitor. A judge who wants the good horse to win will look away just before the good horse's bad bobble, while a judge who wants a good horse to lose will watch the good horse all the way into and through the approaching catastrophe. Judges may or may not deliberately make those now-I-see-it, now-I-don't calculations, but to an owner's watchful eye, judges can sure appear to be doing so as they cast their view here and there about the ring, searching to discover just the right six- or eight-horse finishing order.

Determining the proper finishing order of six or eight performance competitors out of classes as big as twenty, thirty, or even forty horses approaches madness. I did some apprentice judging preparing to qualify for a judge's license for which in the end I never applied. Picking out the better horses is not the challenge in the big classes. One doesn't even find it hard to rank them one through six or eight. The problems arise when better horses start making frequent bobbles that lesser horses don't make. The six best horses may give the six worst performances, and vice versa. Judging performance classes isn't a matter of picking out the best *performer*. Rather, judging a performance class involves picking out the best *performance*. I found myself repeatedly placing horses that I wouldn't want to own or ride above horses that I would want to own and ride, simply because the lesser-talented horses that time gave better performances. Making those two-criteria judgments (talent plus consistency) gets all the harder when a couple of good horses make bad *late* bobbles, too late for the judge to pick out new contenders to take the good horses' places. Even when awarding only six ribbons, one learns to have seventh, eighth, and ninth-place horses in mind right up to the class's end. Or, if one prefers shenanigans, then one looks away from the good horses toward the end of the class so as not to notice anything that upsets the well-developed order.

My wife was an outstanding, elegant, beautiful rider. She always looked better on a horse than I ever looked on a horse. She nonetheless came to believe, with some merit, that she never caught a break in those performance anomalies. If her good horse was going to make a bad bobble in an otherwise strong performance, then the judge was going to be looking *right at her* when the bad bobble happened. She ended up feeling like she won more seconds and thirds than firsts, when she and her horses had first-place talent. Maybe judges just liked looking at her ride. I know that I did. I'd watch her ride around and around on another perfect ride until the very last canter depart, which is the most likely place for a last-minute bobble. Sure enough, the judge would be staring right at her when giving the ringmaster and announcer the signal to take the horses from the walk to the canter. And presto, her horse would do the most-beautiful canter depart—moments *before* the announcer gave the command. Seeing her jaw clench and eyes narrow at the bobble, I'd know better than to ask her later as we walked back to the barn with the red or yellow ribbon if she hadn't somehow given the horse an early signal. She did, though, win her well-earned share of blue ribbons.

An especially large class, like the full forty horses that rules allow, make it hard for a good rider and horse to get noticed. Experienced riders in large classes go to great lengths to get their performance horses into an open space for the judge to see as they whirl past among the sea of other horses. Although show rings are large, horses are herd animals, meaning that they just seem to naturally bunch up notwithstanding their riders' efforts. Going past a judge's view three-deep is not at all unusual in a large class. Horses well off the rail and toward the center of the ring hide from the judge horses on the rail or near the rail. A proper tactic to get away from a clump of horses and take an open place on the rail is to make a circle, although sometimes one just ends up in another clump of horses. Another way is to simply cut across the ring to an open space, although sometimes two or three other riders will simultaneously think of the same thing so that one ends up back in a clump of horses again. One of the nation's best trainers took in these large classes to riding twenty feet in from the rail, always, in a tighter circle than all the other horses. He and his horses got noticed. Other, lesser-skilled riders soon imitated the strategy, some of them comically nearly running down the judge who would occasionally have to leap back from the oncoming horse.

If you think large Arab performance classes can be a spectacle, then you are right. The bigger spectacle, though, is in large Saddlebred shows where these efforts to place one's performance horse in an open spot in front of the judge reach a ridiculous level. Or perhaps Saddlebred riders have hit on the solution to the large-class problem. Saddlebred riders slow, pool, and even stop their tall mounts at each end of the ring, which then allows one at a time to shoot out of the pool and down the other rail past the judge. These queues at each end of the ring are not precise. The beautiful but ungainly Saddlebreds don't stop on a dime when they reach ring's end and don't line up in respectful order behind competitors waiting their turn to shoot down the ring's other side. They instead sort of crash into the pool at ring's end and then sort of shoot back out of the pool whenever their milling about seems to take them to advantageous position. The Saddlebred's very high mechanical action and the lack of agility and control that attends it, together with the Saddlebred's lower intelligence or sensitivity to its rider's precise commands, make the whole affair a comedy, especially when two or three at a time emerge from the pool to shoot down the ring in one another's way or wake, spoiling the intended my-turn-at-the-judge effect. In some of these Saddlebred classes, good horses appear to lose out to bad horses not because the judge can't see them three-deep along the rail but because they never quite got their lone shot down the rail.

Judges usually have a ringmaster on whom to lean in their efforts to keep a class orderly and the show on track. Ringmasters first ensure that the ring's gate opens and closes when it should, a bigger deal than some might anticipate. The practice developed of prominent trainers wanting to be either the first or last in the ring, one supposes to take advantage of primacy and recency effects. A judge almost must pay attention to a contestant making a first grand entrance to much whooping and applause. The ringmaster has the job of keeping order in the gate area and control over opening of the gate, as contestants vie for primacy. Yet some trainers contrarily like to let the other contestants wear themselves out going around and around the ring before they make a last grand entrance to much whooping and applause. The ringmaster has the job of timing how long the gate may remain open and whether a too-late contestant may get in. Once all contestants are in the ring, the ringmaster stands within earshot of the judge to communicate the judge's gait commands to the announcer. The ringmaster also surveys the ring for events that might interrupt the class, like broken gear, a kicking or bucking horse, or a retiring contestant who wishes that the gate open to let them out.

Ringmasters thus play important roles, letting the judge concentrate on the contest. Ringmasters, though, are also part of the show. Some dress only in business-like attire, maybe sport coat and dress slacks or, on a hot day, no coat but still a dress shirt (even if short-sleeved) and tie. But others dress in full regalia, meaning tall black riding boots, white breeches, white shirt with black tie and red vest, long-tailed red coat, and top hat—like a circus ringmaster. They then run dramatically about the ring to command the opening and closing of the gate, at the end of the class sprint the completed judge's card to the announcer, and in between run hither and thither to rescue damsels in distress. If a competitor loses a hat to the wind, then the bright-clad ringmaster dashes in between horses to rescue the hat before a hoof can crush it, cradles it gently in hand for the remainder of the class, and then ceremoniously hands it back to the bare-headed competitor in the lineup at the end of class to the crowd's appreciative applause and laughter. If one is to be a ringmaster in life, then why not dress for and play the full role?

Announcers are also allies to the judge. Announcers give early first, second, and third calls for each class on a public-address system back to the barn area to help competitors get ready. Then, when the judge is ready and not before, the announcer calls the class, identifying it for the crowd and ensuring that competitors milling outside the ring know that they are entering the correct class. Neophyte competitors sometimes end up in the wrong class, slinking back out the gate as soon as they realize, to make another entry, surely less confident and grand, in the next class. Performance horses enter at a jog for Western classes and trot for park, English, and driving horses, the gait that gets the competitors quickly, but not too chaotically, into the ring. On the judge's word and ringmaster's signal, the announcer then calls gait changes entailing walk, trot, and canter in each direction in English and park classes, walk, jog trot, and lope (slower canter) in Western classes, and extended trot and hand gallop in English mature-horse and championship classes. Classes entail some drama when the announcer gives the call to *reverse* from one direction to the other, usually at a trot, when horses must cut across the ring to head in the opposite direction. The drama involves who impedes, cuts off, or upstages whom, or nearly runs over the judge or ringmaster, in cutting across the ring. The peril is especially great for buggy classes where horses could spook, wheels could lock, and a wreck ensue.

An announcer's other main role beyond giving class and gait commands involves reading the winning order. The announcement at smaller shows usually proceeds from first to last, giving the first-place finisher a chance to pose for a ring-center photo. The announcement at larger shows and regional and National Championships proceeds from last to first, increasing the anticipation. Announcers must pronounce each horse's name, not an easy task for Egyptian, Polish, or Spanish names popular among those strains of Arabian horses, and names, like my horse Zzyzx, which announcers almost never got right. Some announcers play up their role, adding humorous quips here and there. One Indiana announcer with an especially good voice and timing developed such a good reputation for keeping shows lighthearted and fun that the National Championships retained him. Oddly, his homespun Indiana humor didn't play so well at the hoity-toity National Championships, which didn't renew his retainer. They wanted ritzy but got rustic, posh but got poor.

At smaller shows, judge, ringmaster, announcer, and show secretary bundle into a ringside show booth, from which the show secretary runs the show and where the judge and ringmaster retire between classes to take shelter from rain and sun. Major shows make a center stage in the ring, sometimes with just yellow rope, red rope stands or stakes, and ornamental bushes, other times with a small raised platform and white tent covering. There, the show's small community of judges, ringmasters, announcer, and show secretary huddle for the three or four days, or for National Championships the full week, of the show. In its own way, the central stage entertains the crowd, as judges in tuxedos or long dresses, ringmasters in their bright long-tailed coats, and announcers and show secretaries in business or formal attire busy themselves with the show's administration, doubtless mixed with occasional social chatter. Owners, family members, friends, trainers, and grooms who watch the beautifully dressed officials enjoy themselves running the show from center ring imagine their own elevation to such high station, with the élan of Clark Gable and Bette Davis, or Fred Astaire and Ginger Rogers.

16

Transport

Horse transport is essential to horse world. One would get nowhere with horses in the way that we use them in modern society if one could not move them about the country with reasonable safety and efficiency. Training horses entails moving horses from owner's farm to training stable and back again once trained. Breeding horses entails moving mares from owner's farm to stallion's location and, once bred and safely in foal, back again to the mare's farm for foaling. Showing horses entails moving horses from farm to show and from show to show before back to farm. Buying and selling horses entails moving horses from the seller's farm to the buyer's farm, if not also from seller's farm to auction place to buyer's farm. For all these purposes, horses regularly move from East Coast to West Coast and from Midwest to Southeast or Southwest, or the reverse, and then back again. Horses are constantly crisscrossing the country. Horses also move from continent to continent. Every trainer and groom has abundant experience with and many stories about transporting horses.

Check the parking lot of a major horse show, or even stop at a major truck stop in an area like Lexington where horse farms concentrate, and you will see the various transport means. Most involve some sort of vehicle and trailer, although horse vans are common and popular in certain regions and breeds. Six-horse vans, in which the cab, engine, and trailer box are all on a single two-axle frame, are common for dressage stables. When my wife and I had our public training stable at a dressage farm, we often rented its six-horse van for shows, generally the only van to appear at our Midwest-region shows for Arabian horses, although Arab trainers on the East Coast were then using some six-horse vans. The six-horse vans have the convenience of a single piece of equipment, but their single-frame design requires the trailer floor to be higher, making the ramp up which horses must walk steeper, and requiring sideboards to the ramp. Given the steep ramp, trainers can find loading a six-horse van more difficult than loading a trailer. The horses look a little like mountain goats as they lean way forward and clamor up the ramp. We once had a young horse clamor up the ramp fine, but when time came to lead back down that steep ramp, she took a long look, shivered, and then leapt to the bottom at once, landing spread-eagle. Not the best move.

One must also take greater care driving the tipsy, high-center-of-gravity van around corners. Cornering is a big deal for horses. The stalls in a van or trailer are necessarily narrow, just wide enough to squeeze in the horse. In most vans and trailers, the horses face forward or rearward, meaning that at every corner, the horses tend to tip side to side, leaning if necessary up against the side rails. A horse's long, narrow wheelbase (a vehicle term, but you get the picture) makes cornering even tipsier for them. Take a corner too fast, and the leaning horse panics, scrambling against the sides of the narrow stall for footing. When novice owners arrive at the training stable or showgrounds with their new horse and trailer, you will sometimes hear the horses scrambling frantically against the trailer's sides as the owner drives them around corners. Bad driving can spoil a horse for trailering. One never quite knows what is going on back in the trailer as one hurtles down the highway. Sometimes, a driver can hear or sense the horses scrambling, struggling, or kicking. The van or truck and trailer may surge and fishtail. In such cases, wise drivers stop to check the horses. Incredibly, we once had a horse facing backward in a two-horse trailer next to another horse, when we arrived back home from an exhibition with it. To this day, I have no idea how that horse got itself unhooked at the head and squeezed all the way around in a stall no wider than the horse was. We simply walked around the back of the trailer, and there the horse was, hanging its head out the back, despite that we had sensed no commotion along the way.

Much more common than vans for horse transport are trailers, all the way from the tiny two-horse trailers that mom and dad can pull with their family vehicle if it has a decent engine, suspension, and frame, to the gooseneck nine- and even twelve-horse trailers pulled behind dual-wheel pickup trucks and semi-tractor trailers. Most trainers take responsibility for transporting their stable's horses, in part because transport that owners pay per mile can be a profit center. Trainers may get horses to a show in a hodgepodge of vehicles and trailers. Most trainers either own or have ready access to one large trailer of some kind, for between six to twelve horses, but may supplement the big rig with two- and four-horse trailers. Some horses, especially stallions, just haul better alone. In smaller rigs, horses often stand two by two, perhaps all four or six horses entering from the rear of the trailer to face forward, two by two behind one another, requiring that they back out. In larger rigs, horses often stand three by three and may enter three from the back and six from a side door, with the three in the back facing forward but the six in the middle facing one another.

My first big rig had a beat-up old eight-horse trailer pulled by an old but serviceable International Harvester cab-over tractor with a sleeper. My parents bought the rig for a song and had a training client of mine reconfigure the trailer and paint the tractor and trailer. The client, a car-wash owner who was a gifted mechanic and welder, had a mare to train for his children to show. He would spend hours cutting and welding on the old trailer while I trained his mare and helped his kids. He did an incredible job on the rig, which proved a wise purchase. The biggest thing I'd driven until then was a pickup truck with a four-horse gooseneck trailer. The old International Harvester tractor had ten forward gears on a five-hole shifter with a hi-lo button attached to it. I first drove the tractor in a parking lot to get used to sitting so high above the road, cranking on the big horizontal steering wheel without power steering, and accelerating through the odd shifter-button-shifter-button sequence to get from first gear low through first high, second low, second high, and so on. That much wasn't so hard. The harder part was getting the engine speed just right with the accelerator pedal for every gear change. Depressing the clutch pedal didn't make any difference. You'd still grind the gears even with the clutch pedal down if you hadn't used the accelerator pedal to feather the engine speed back to just the right point.

Driving a big rig is fun and a privilege—for a while. Roaring up through Georgia high above the freeway in a cab-over tractor, spouse asleep in the bunk behind you, jammed in the middle of a caravan of eighteen wheelers flying along through the middle of the night, is intoxicating. Like many things, though, the fun can wear off, considering the jolts from the potholes and the weary arms, neck, and shoulders from cranking the big wheel back and forth. The best moment then is hearing the sharp hiss when you set the emergency brake at the end of a long run and tumble out of the tractor to solid ground. The feeling after an especially long drive is a bit like getting off a boat after hours or days at sea. You must get your land legs back. We made some long runs. I drove a four-horse gooseneck trailer across the country thirty-nine hours straight following my mentor's nine-horse big rig. We stopped halfway to try to catch an hour's nap, but no one could sleep, so we just got back in and headed the last eighteen hours home. That drive took a few days from which to recover.

The gorgeously named and designed *Streamliner* was then the premier big rig, looking somewhat like those sleek stainless-steel *Airstream* camper trailers but much bigger and with prim stainless-steel horizontal ribs. For a while, each prominent trainer tried to outdo the other with a newer, bigger, and sleeker *Streamliner,* doubtless making the *Streamliner* salesperson rich and happy. The rig's high cost and glamorous beauty made a big deal out of parking it in just the right highly visible spot at each show grounds. No one should have been surprised about the trailer competition because showing horses is itself a look-at-me sort of sport. The fancier big rigs added to the mystique of transporting horses. I don't know how truckers who long-haul rotting produce, steel rolls, car parts, cement barriers, and other stuff feel about their work, but hauling horses must differ at least somewhat. Horse-hauling is not like hauling chickens, cattle, or hogs destined for the meat market. Horses are precious cargo, living and breathing pieces of rideable art. Regular truckers undoubtedly recognize the difference, treating the fancy horse vans like they might treat a busload of rich tourists. But when the trainer tumbles wearily out of the rig's driver seat at a truck stop in the middle of the night to walk bow-legged across the parking lot, the stop's regular truckers still grudgingly acknowledge the truck-driver fellowship.

Strange things appear when hauling horses across the country's wastelands through the middle of the night. My wife and I were heading along the freeway south from Albuquerque at about three in the morning, driving a dual-cab, dual-wheel pickup pulling six horses in a gooseneck trailer on the long southern route to Tucson and back up to Scottsdale. New Mexico claims itself the Land of Enchantment, as it was that crisp, starry, moonlit night. Everything around was pitch black, with no other traffic whatsoever except for headlights on the freeway up ahead from a vehicle that didn't seem to be moving. We slowed as we approached the stationary headlights until we reached the vehicle, lights on, engine running, parked diagonally across both lanes of the freeway, with no driver or other occupant anywhere in sight. In the moonlight, we could clearly see nothing around for miles but barren land, no one in sight, just the empty vehicle sitting running in the middle of the freeway as we pulled to the shoulder and made our way around and on. Scotty must have beamed the driver aboard.

My wife and I had never seen anything on the highway quite so hair-raising strange. That same trip also produced an epic highway moment, one that neither of us will ever forget. We had started out in Northern Indiana, stopped in Oklahoma City at the horse motel for some rest, and were once again driving from Oklahoma City to Scottsdale, a long but doable haul. Then a snowstorm hit as we made our way across the Texas Panhandle and into Northern New Mexico. The driving worsened the farther we pushed on through the building hills and low mountain ranges toward Albuquerque, as night fell. Then, we crested one of those low ranges with a sigh of relief, only to see ahead of us a two-mile-long twisted string of brake lights and taillights, cars, trucks, and trailers strewn left and right on and off the freeway, down at the bottom of the valley and all the way up the next range. We could see vehicles trying unsuccessfully to get up and out of the valley on its far side, cars sliding this way and that way, trucks jackknifing their trailers as they skidded backward down the freeway. We had only two choices: pull over and wait hours, maybe all night or for days, for wreckers coming from who-knows-where to clear the valley, or descend into the valley's vehicular hell, joining the melee with only a one-in-a-hundred chance of emerging up the other side and over the next crest to discover who-knows-what of more wreckage in valleys beyond.

Down into the valley we headed, skating along the ice-covered freeway just fast enough for some momentum to carry up the next range but not so fast as to lose control of the gooseneck or be unable to avoid a spinning car or jackknifed truck and trailer. Incredibly, we made it across the long valley floor without having to break much momentum, cars and trucks miraculously having stayed out of the way. But now, would we make it up the long climb over the next range? The dual-wheel pickup and gooseneck slowed on the long climb until having spent the last of our precarious little momentum. We were doomed to come to a halt and start the slide back down the long climb like the other cars and trucks in the ditches on both sides or scattered along the shoulder, or so we thought. Miraculously, though, the dual wheels somehow took slight hold. I nursed the accelerator so as not to spin the rear wheels and lose all hope of continuing the creeping climb. A path cleared ahead, cars and trucks giving up hope and pulling to the right lane or left bit of shoulder. We reached the crest at a crawl but made it, leaving behind the long dark valley of desperation. I don't even remember the rest of what we encountered through the mountain ranges into Albuquerque, but we made it without incident, pulling into an all-night diner at around 1 a.m. to reconnoiter. To avoid more of the snowstorm, we would take the southern route down to Las Cruces, over to Tucson, and back up into Phoenix. Better safe, long, tired, and late than sorry.

I had the odd fortune of seeing much of America from the back of a horse trailer, too. On some of my mentor trainer's trips around the country, we would haul horses so valuable, young, old, scared of trailers, or ornery that having someone ride in the back of the trailer with the horses seemed like a good idea. I never minded it. Sitting in a tractor-trailer cab high over the highway is an adventure and privilege. Driving a dual-wheel pickup truck hauling horses is likewise a relative ease, if the weather isn't kicking butt and the traffic is reasonable. But standing or sitting in the back of a horse van flying along the freeways is like riding a magic carpet. If the horses are peacefully munching hay, then one can look out the open upper doors, smelling the fresh air, fresh hay, and horse breath while watching the endless scenery rush by, almost as if one was standing at the barn door looking outside. Most of the time, the horses, though hurtling along the freeway while standing up, are relaxed and oblivious. I used to take along a book or two and a sack of snacks, sitting comfortably in a deck chair, with the only annoyance trying to

Yee-Haw!

keep the horses from blowing their snot on me, which they seem to do quite often in the trailer with their muzzles buried in a hay bag. Maybe it's hay fever. My mentor trainer and any other grooms along for the ride would laugh at my reading, especially when it was something like a fine-arts text my brother had left over from college.

Not every trip, though, is idyllic for the horses. America's highways are dangerous, with tens of thousands dying in accidents on them every year. I was in motor-vehicle accidents twice hauling horses. The first time, we had just finished a three-day show in a Central Ohio town and were heading the four-hour drive home, when a tiny car pulled out right in front of me and then promptly stopped on the two-lane road, waiting for traffic to pass before turning left. I stomped on the pickup truck's brakes, but the gooseneck trailer's brakes never took hold (they were fitful at times), and with the truck brakes alone I could only slow the ungainly rig before it bumped the tiny vehicle out of the way. The horses were unhurt, not even shaken. A groom asleep in the gooseneck wasn't even sure if anything had happened. But the pickup truck's radiator had a little hole in it, the tiny car's rear end didn't look so good, and the local police wanted assurance that the seventeen-year-old driver (me) would pay the ticket that they promptly issued when arriving on the scene. Thankfully, a mechanic came out to his radiator shop just down the road to fix the pickup's leak, and after taking me to the station, the police relented and took a check. We were two hours late getting home.

The other accident wasn't so pretty. My wife and I had just left the Kentucky Horse Park with another pickup truck and gooseneck at around 5 a.m. the Monday after a four-day show, hoping to be home to Northern Indiana by late day. I pulled the rig onto the freeway entrance ramp and then merged onto the vacant freeway, climbing up a long hill adjacent to the Horse Park at a little more than the minimum freeway speed, which was all that the pickup truck could muster up the hill without any freeway momentum yet. We hadn't even gotten out of the Horse Park's sight when the rig suddenly surged violently forward, so hard that the pickup's front-seat bench in which we sat bent back. An eighteen-wheeler had slammed into the back of our gooseneck trailer. I pulled the limping rig far off the shoulder and ran back to see how the horses were. God bless him, the trucker was already at the gooseneck's side gate, apologizing and ready to help. He and I let the gate down and immediately saw that the two horses who had been in the rear stalls now had their forelegs up over the chest gate in front of them. The collision had catapulted them up and over the four-foot-high barrier. Somehow, together we heaved the horses back over the gates so that we could open the gates and lead them out of the rear-crushed trailer. The abashed trucker, twice my weight, did more of the necessary heaving than I did.

Outside the trailer in the foggy dawn, we could tell that only one of the horses that had been in the trailer's rear section facing forward was hurt. None of the other four horses, three facing backward in the front section and the other one that had been in the rear and shoved over the gate, was hurt. Unfortunately, the rear horse, a black two-year-old colt, had a cut on the rear fetlock area that required stitches and healed with a significant scar. He may have suffered other injury to the hind end and legs because he thereafter just didn't carry himself right, as we learned when we tried to resume showing him later that summer. At the scene, though, we soon had a vet to the freeway shoulder, where we tended to the colt's injury. A commercial horse hauler was on the scene not too long later, and we unloaded and loaded the five horses into its trailer for the reconfigured ride home. A wrecker hauled away the crippled gooseneck, leaving my wife and I to drive the now-lonely dual-cab, dual-wheel pickup truck home. With the seat bent back, and the two of us peering up and over the dashboard, we felt like we were cruising along the strip in a low-rider. In all, things worked out about as well as they could. I felt bad for the trucker who admitted that he had been drowsy in the early morning dawn after a night-long haul. He doubtless had a lot to explain to the investigating police officer and to his employer.

For decades after leaving horse world, I dreamt of horses, dreams that only in the past decade somewhat abated. Those who study dreams say that dream horses represent spirits. Most of my horse dreams entailed struggles with horses, indeed, nightmares with fearsome, morphing, phantasmagoric horses. Perhaps not surprisingly given the stories just retold, many of those nightmares involved hauling horses. I strongly suspect, though, that the cause of the horse-hauling nightmares was neither bad weather nor accidents but instead the challenges we faced hauling *stallions*. Recall that stallions accidentally getting loose together will try to kill one another, with one stallion or the other promptly or soon succeeding. Stallions in the wild are either king of the mare harem or somewhere off alone in the distance plotting to take over the harem. Yet hauling horses to shows frequently entails stuffing stallions into those tiny trailer or van stalls right next to other horses and facing the front or rear of still other horses. Under those close-quarter circumstances, stallions tend to go berserk, roaring, kicking, striking, biting, and clamoring until tamed with chain, twitch, club, or strong sedative. Hauling stallions is not for the faint hearted.

One incident exemplified the challenges. I had caravanned following my mentor trainer from Michigan to Oklahoma City on the way to National Championships in Albuquerque. My mentor was hauling his breeder/owner's prized five-year-old imported Egyptian stallion Assad along with several other stallions and mares, some of them also imported, all of them champions, and all of them highly valuable. Assad had won every halter class and championship he had so far entered and would go on to win National Champion stallion in Albuquerque. Assad was already breeding dozens of mares and would breed the maximum allowed for the next couple of years after his National Championship win. My mentor trainer had done an exquisite job of fitting Assad for the coming National Championship. Among many other things, we had trotted him in a bitting rig for miles along dirt roads behind a pickup truck, building his stamina. Assad got every special grain, every special supplement, every special brushing, every special massage, everything, to bring him to his greatest strength and beauty. Between the breeding, fitting, and feeding, Assad was one spectacular handful. Yet my mentor had somehow to haul him in the trailer next to and facing the other mares and stallions on their way to the National Championship.

We somehow made it without incident to Oklahoma City, where we put the horses in the horse motel overnight. But by the time we loaded the horses again the next morning, Assad was having none of it. Before we got just a mile or two down the freeway, Assad had put his front hooves up in the feed area where his head should have been, in a screaming effort to kill or breed the horse hidden by a small plywood barrier just in front of him. Assad was in the back end of the nine-horse trailer, meaning that he faced forward, with a narrow feed area with sliding plywood doors hiding the horse that had loaded from the trailer's center and was facing backward toward him. Assad couldn't see the horse beside him or in front of him (plywood barriers wisely separated the horses each into their own little stall), but he could sure smell and hear them, because they were only a foot or two away. My mentor could tell from the trailer's surging and swaying that something bad was going on in the back of the trailer and so, fortunately, had pulled to the shoulder. Along the freeway's shoulder, with morning rush-hour traffic hurling by, my mentor and I climbed up through the little door that allowed access to the narrow little feed area separating Assad's roaring head from the other horse that was facing him across the little feed area.

My mentor somehow yelled, harassed, chain-jerked, and beat Assad back until Assad had his front hooves back down on the trailer floor. He then recruited me (a groom that my mentor had brought along had already failed in this difficult role) to sit on an upside-down bucket in the little elevated feed area with a chain on Assad, a little twitch club, and as much courage as I could muster to try to keep Assad back on the floor. My mentor's wife took over driving the gooseneck rig in which I had followed my mentor. For the next couple of hours, as the caravan resumed, I sat on the bucket hollering at Assad every time that he roared and tried to get his front hooves back up in the tiny little feed area where I sat, to get at the horse behind me. The groom that my mentor had brought along sat nearby on the other side of the little feed area, watching me while learning how to keep a twelve-hundred-pound stallion from ripping your head off to get at a horse behind you. The arrangement worked. When we stopped for a break about one-hundred miles down the freeway, the groom took over my role, and I got back into my gooseneck rig to drive the rest of the way to Albuquerque. Fortunately, Assad had only a little cut on the front of one pastern, a barely noticeable wound that in the last few days before his winning National Championship received the maximum care and attention.

While this event may sound dramatic, stallions wreaking trailer havoc was common. Some stallions would haul fine next to a gelding, even seeming to appreciate the companionship. They might even haul reasonably well with mares and fillies, once one got the stallion safely into its stall and the curtains or other dividers drawn so that they were no longer nose-to-nose with the mare or filly, as would be necessary to navigate the stallion into the trailer. But haul two stallions or a colt and a stallion? Now we're talking mayhem. After a show or two, a trainer gets to know how much or little each stallion tolerates. We would soon discover different loading partners and patterns that somehow lessened a new stallion's roaring tomfoolery and gradually reduced the different means of desperate restraint. Sometimes a curtain was enough, or maybe extra feed. Sometimes, though, a groom had to ride all the way at the stallion's head with a chain on the stallion's halter, ensuring that the stallion didn't even *think* of it. Sedatives, difficult to control and trust, were a last-ditch remedy. I will never, *never* miss hauling stallions.

One transport obligation that I somehow missed that I do in somewhat regret missing, though, was flying a horse into the country from Cairo, Egypt. My mentor had flown many imported Egyptian Arabians into the country for the magnate for whom he worked. At one point, my mentor had one more to import, a filly that had somehow stayed behind. He asked me to make the trip over for the filly and to ride in the cargo plane with it back to quarantine at a U.S. destination. I got my passport all set and was ready to go when my mentor's schedule cleared so that he could make the trip instead. I was disappointed for having missed the adventure until I heard when he got back that he had been taken from the plane and held at gunpoint for several hours on a North African layover until suitable financial arrangements had been made, evidently involving wiring money to satisfy the demand. I hadn't looked forward to that kind of adventure. Indeed, my mentor could walk and talk his way out of anything, even when others couldn't understand his heavy rural-Virginia accent, as I am sure that the North Africans who held him couldn't understand him. Me? I'd still be in North Africa or, more likely, dead. I just wanted to see how a horse reacted to takeoff.

17

Farriers

Farriers form an oddball profession out of an ancient craft that has no value to a modern economy but nonetheless is essential for anyone owning a horse. That irony of being members of the most-eccentric of seemingly useless professions but knowing their critical worth may be what makes farriers so quirky. I suppose that some farriers may be perfectly normal, like the person next door who designs and troubleshoots supply chains for an automotive manufacturer, works nine to five, and takes out the garbage every Wednesday precisely at six. But if any such normal-seeming farriers exist, then I sure haven't met one. They are instead hippy orphans of the back-to-nature sixties, trimming horse hooves as a natural vocation that earns them just enough unreported cash to buy medicinal smoke. Or they are Steampunk engineers who never made out it out of the 1800s and so still love to forge, bang, and twist iron into fire pokers, fence posts, and horseshoes. Or they are horse whisperers who can sweet-talk a frightened little filly into gently entrusting her deadly quick back hoof into their powerful hands wielding steel nippers but who otherwise can't teach a horse to walk. To be reasonably dedicated and any good at their arduous, dirty, sweaty, dangerous, and incredibly picky and precise craft, farriers must love the out-of-the-way, old-fashioned, tough, and eccentric.

At most farms, the farrier is the most-beloved character of the whole bunch including trainers, apprentices, owners, grooms, veterinarians, family members, and friends. Horse hooves grow at constant rate, like fingernails. You know how you clip your nails one day, and before you know it, they need clipping again? The same thing happens with horse hooves. You get eight good weeks, maybe ten, and you need the farrier back again. A busy training stable will have the farrier visit about every four weeks to divide and spread out the work. When the farrier visits, much else must stop, as trainer or groom retrieves horse after horse, and trainer and farrier inspect hooves and consult. If a groom is around to hold each horse as the farrier works, then the trainer may be able to sneak off and work a horse here and there between consults. But sometimes, the team finds it more efficient for the groom to work and the trainer to hold horses to consult, giving the trainer a rare day off from training and making for a sort of busman's holiday. Some trainers love the farrier's visit, even if the trainer isn't getting much else done.

Indeed, sometimes the trainer must restrain a horse, like weanlings getting hooves trimmed for the first time or yearlings or other young horses getting shod for the first time and frightened of or objecting to the farrier's work. Even horses that farriers have trimmed or shod many times sometimes fight the work, fidgeting, hopping about on three legs as the farrier holds the fourth leg, and trying to jerk the held leg free. These movements can easily seriously hurt the farrier, who wields and repeatedly uses a razor-sharp hoof knife. A horse's jerk of the hoof at just the wrong moment, and the knife can cut a finger or hand just as easily as the hoof's sole. Shoeing likewise entails delicate and dangerous moments, like when the farrier uses forge tongs to burn a trim pattern in the hoof's sole with a blazing-hot shoe. Farriers get burned a lot. The most-delicate moment of shoeing, though, is when the farrier has hammered three or four nails into one side of the shoe, leaving the sharp nail points sticking through the hoof's side wall. The farrier must nip the sharp points off with metal cutters before the horse can jerk the hoof free, sticking the nail points into the farrier's hand or leg. You've never seen a farrier work so fast and sweat so much as when hammering the shoe nails through a frightened yearling's hoof and nimbly nipping them off.

In case you hadn't figured it out, farriers trim and shoe horse hooves in a precarious position. They must hold the horse's front hoof *between their legs*, or in the case of a back hoof cup the hoof between the legs while holding the back leg up over their hip. To do so, the farrier must stand backward to the horse and face down at the hoof, an awkward position that requires a sort of standing squat extremely stressful on the farrier's lower back. All farriers have back problems, which may further explain their eccentricity as they resort to various licit and illicit pain remedies and true or manufactured excuses for not showing up. One of my favorite farriers, also one of the least reliable, soon let on that he kept on his truck's sun visor a list of excuses for why he was late or had not shown up. The down-and-backward position also leaves the farrier unaware and vulnerable to just about everything going on around the farrier, including bites from the horse. Cross ties, running a line from either side of the halter to either side of a hallway wall, is the preferred method for restraining a horse for the farrier, but not every horse stands for cross ties. The trainer or a skilled handler may end up holding the horse.

Trimming a horse can take from fifteen to thirty minutes, depending on the farrier's speed and extent of the work. Shoeing a horse invariably takes more like an hour. Not every horse gets shod. Breeders shoe few, while trainers need most horses shod. Horses only need shoes when you work them, especially on hard ground where their hooves will wear unevenly or on ground with gravel and stones that will chip off the hoof wall. Young horses running free, mares kept only for breeding, and old horses out to pasture don't need shoes. Trail horses ridden a time or two a week may not need shoes unless the trails are rocky. Show horses are uniformly shod, at least when two or three years old and older. One rarely shod a yearling until yearling competitions grew in significance with money coming into the breed, and trainers and owners realized that shoes add a little to the yearling's stature and action. Horses do throw shoes, even in the show ring, making a farrier a necessity at the shows, sometimes at Saddlebred shows for a dramatic re-shoeing in the ring.

You may not know this fact, but dogs crave the trimmings of horse hooves like cats fall for catnip. A horse should bear its weight on the hoof's perimeter and frog (the softer center-back of the hoof), not the sole, which should instead be concave. Thus after filing the hoof's wall and sole down with a coarse file (a first way of accomplishing the trimming for which the owner hires the farrier), farriers then slice off thin wafers of the hoof's sole with their hoof knife until they have carved the necessary hollow. Dogs will watch the wafers fly and grab one if they can, chewing and swallowing it like a delicious slice of heaven. Better, though, are the hoof walls that the farrier then nips off, working the farrier's way around the hoof-wall perimeter with the nippers. The nipped hoof-wall pieces have more substance than the flying wafers. A dog will give its right paw for one, darting in and out with the first rich find. A stalking and darting dog can disturb a horse whose hoof a farrier holds, which can disturb the farrier trying vainly to hold onto the spooked and hopping horse's hoof. So, a wise farrier will toss the first good nip of hoof wall to a waiting dog so that the dog need not stalk and dart. A wise dog will then slink away to chew on, soften, and soon swallow the hoof wall.

Dogs stalk and dart for hoof pieces because dog owners quickly learn that horse hoof does not digest. Dogs vomit every bit of horse hoof that they so deliriously ingest, which makes the dog's owner yell at and chase the dog away from the farrier, which explains the dog's stalking and darting to avoid the owner's discovery, which explains the farrier tossing pieces of hoof to the slinking dog. Dog owners try to sweep up and securely dispose of the slices of hoof sole and chunks of nipped hoof wall as quickly as they fall from the farrier's work, which just causes the dogs to watch more closely and act more quickly to grab a piece before the shovel scoops up the pile and the pile disappears into the garbage can. Dogs that aren't very good at the darting and dodging learn to bully or sweet-talk the darting dogs out of hoof bits. This circus of catch-as-catch-can is all part of the fun of the farrier's visit. Even the dogs love the farrier. Dogs have even been known to knock over garbage cans to recover and abscond with the hidden treasure, although in that effort they may have help from raccoons or cats. Despite best clean-up efforts, the dogs rediscover and vie for bits of hoof here and there about the barn for days after a farrier's visit.

Like any tradesperson or professional, farriers vary in their skill. The best are artists with the hoof knife and nippers, and craftsman with the forge, hammer, and shoe. Unlike shoes for humans, horseshoes don't just come in every necessary size and style, off the rack. Farriers must shape a shoe to fit each hoof, either from a stock horseshoe or, in rare cases, out of a rectangle bar of steel. Each hoof is a little different. A farrier could nail a stock shoe to the hoof's sole and then file the hoof wall to fit, but the hoof wall is only so thick, and while some light filing for final fit is standard, the shoe must fit the hoof, not the other way around. Thus, the first thing that a farrier must do on arriving at the stable to do some shoeing is heat up the small gas-fired forge in the back of the farrier's pickup truck or van. The forge must get hot enough to turn the stock horseshoe glowing orange for the farrier to work into the right shape with the hammer on the anvil. Yes, they still do it that way, bang after bang on the anvil, and back and forth between the forge and testing the fit on the hoof, until the shoe is near enough to nail to the hoof before a final light filing of the hoof wall for perfect fit.

The anvil artistry increases considering horseshoe options. The basic shoe is just the curved piece of steel shaped to fit the hoof wall. But then, a horse's great weight and violent hoof strikes can force shoes out of place on the hoof sole. As a remedy, a farrier may bang out of the stock horseshoe two toe clips to hold the shoe in place. Some trainers like the rear of a shoe to fold over into a little clip to augment the hoof's rolling action, like human running shoes that encourage an efficient foot strike. Sleigh horses used on snow and ice in winter must have forged gripping points. Some horses need protection or support across the back of the hoof, calling for a bar shoe—in essence, a shoe that goes all the way around the hoof instead of just around the front-and-side wall. Some horses need greater protection of the frog area in the back-middle of the hoof, calling for a heart-bar shoe. Stock horses (Western horses running patterns for show) win by making a twenty-or-longer-foot slide at the end of their runs. The rear hooves of stock horses may thus have sliding shoes with wide surfaces on which to slide, although in a poor trade-off, the slippery back shoes make the horse look like it is trying to run on ice for the rest of the stock-horse pattern.

A good farrier is not just an artist and engineer making attractive and functional shoes but also a physical therapist. A horse is only as good as its legs, and legs remain straight and sound only on level and sound hooves. Judges line up and stare at a horse's front and back legs to ensure that they are plumb straight from the front and rear. By slightly tipping a hoof's sole in or out, a good farrier can make a mildly pigeon-toed or splay-footed horse stand square. Overdo the in-or-out tipping, though, and the farrier will turn a sound horse lame. Farriers must thus strike a delicate balance between making a crooked-legged horse look good on one hand and keeping it functional on the other hand. Farriers often do that delicate work of judging how far to push a leg-stressing cosmetic remedy, in close consultation with the trainer. Judges also watch from front and rear how a horse's legs move, straight in line with the horse's forward motion as desired or instead swinging in or out in unsound pattern. Shoe weights, like the leads on a vehicle wheel rim that balance a tire, can slightly improve the pattern, once again making a farrier the trainer's ally and judge's charlatan.

Farriers also take the upper hand in diagnosing hoof diseases. Horse hooves can get hidden abscesses that lame a horse and threaten its survival. A good farrier can detect an abscess from heat or softness in the trimmed sole and, in some cases, expose the abscess with additional knife work and help treat the abscess with antiseptic-soaked cotton wadding and a rubber pad under the shoe. Horses can also get deadly laminitis from a variety of causes, the effect of which is to trap heat in the leg and hoof and cause the hoof wall to separate. While horses that survive it don't entirely recover from laminitis, a good farrier may be able to trim the affected hooves in ways to ease pain, reduce wear, preserve the hoof, and improve mobility. A good farrier, working closely with a good veterinarian, can in these cases mean the difference between a horse's continued life or euthanasia. Trainers need a good farrier, and farriers know it. Trainers try to give their best farriers the best treatment, of which some farriers take unfortunate advantage. When baby needs new shoes, baby needs new shoes. If a horse's hooves are beginning to exceed the four-and-a-half-inch show limit, then the trainer must find a farrier, even if that means a quick shoe job from a strange farrier at the showgrounds.

Trainers can appreciate a farrier's visit for other reasons than getting a rare break from arduous training *and* completing a critical trimming or re-shoeing. Training on a hot summer day can be brutal. Standing in front of a large fan while holding a horse for the farrier, and watching the farrier sweat like a hog, is a lot cooler and easier. Likewise, training on a bitter winter day can be brutal on the face and fingers. Standing near the blazing-hot forge while holding a horse for the farrier is a lot warmer and easier. The ease increases with the good talk and a cold drink in summers or hot coffee in winter. Farriers get all the gossip as they travel from farm to farm and stable to stable. Farrier visits can be a good opportunity for a trainer to catch up on network developments, even to learn a trick or two about what other trainers are up to. But the big hidden benefit of farrier visits isn't the scuttlebutt or tips. Rather, the hidden benefit is sharing simple fellowship with someone in a different trade or profession serving in the same field. Farrier days are like vet visits, or chatting with the driver who drops off the sacks of grain, or listening to the farmer who delivers the hay. For the horse trainer, farrier days are one of those brief interludes in the daily grind when one realizes that the shared work, no matter where it leads, is enough, rediscovering evidence of a deeper faith in one's steady perseverance.

18

Vets

Like farriers, veterinarians supply essential services to horse farms and training stables. And like farriers, veterinarians are entrepreneurs, generally sole practitioners or at most partners with one or two other vets, serving a regular clientele of horse owners, breeders, and trainers, often remarkably faithfully. Vets get to know their horse patients a little like internists get to know their human patients. Vets also get to know the practices of their stables and farms, and habits of the trainers and breeders who run them. Because of that familiarity, breeders and trainers don't want frequent turnover in vets. Better to stick with one vet who knows a horse's history, symptoms, and peculiarities and the peculiar environment of the stable or farm than to deal with a new and strange veterinarian without any knowledge of history and practice. Horse health depends not only on the horse's physiology but also on the feed, exercise, bedding, ventilation, stress, and other environmental factors around it. A good vet keeps a pulse not just on each horse patient but also on the goings on around the stable or farm.

Large-animal vets differ from small-animal vets in that the former travel in well-equipped trucks from farm to farm while the latter work solely and delicately in an office, not deigning to touch a horse or cow. Most vets do one or the other, small-animal or large-animal practice, not both, although country vets having a large-animal practice may still treat a dog or cat along the way or back in a simple office. Large-animal vets all tend to have the same vehicle, a pickup-truck frame with a specially designed bed insert. The bed insert has one large white-fiberglass lid to raise for access to all sorts of medicines and devices, with additional drawers at the back for more novel vet stuff. The thing smells of antiseptic, rubber hose, and chemical worm medicine. When the vet-truck pulls up, everything is business, serious and expensive business.

Although their services are similarly essential, veterinarians differ in character from farriers in remarkable degree. Vets are university educated, while farriers are generally not, although a few eccentric farriers may have Ph.Ds. in medieval history, extinct languages, or the like. Vets are state-licensed and regulated, while farriers may be wanted by the state for child support or back taxes but otherwise have no need for or interest in dealing with government or civilization. Vets are scientists, while farriers may more generally take interest in ancient or archaic arts, certainly forging but maybe also tattoos, leatherworking, and astrology. Vets hurry from farm to farm, maximizing their personal human capital, the investment that they put in their expensive and extensive education. Farriers, having made no educational investment beyond having hung around a mentor farrier long enough to pick up the simple trade, linger around their beat-up old truck telling stories while the forge cools, hoping not to make it to the next farm that day so that their aching back can take a late afternoon at the bar and a good night's sleep to recover. Don't bother trying to make small talk with a large-animal vet. They're too professional and busy. Make your small talk with the farrier whom you will likely find entertaining and funny.

Veterinarians visit horse farms and training stables for two very different reasons: routine care or life-saving emergency. The routine care of a veterinarian is important to any farm or stable, even if that significance is not immediately evident. From a distance, horses are pastoral objects, tending to look peaceful and healthy, hardly in need of veterinary care. But on closer inspection, the keen eye of a trainer or astute breeder sees needs in a horse's rib-showing, pot-bellied, weedy and reedy condition, or in a horse's voracious appetite but inability to put muscle on the bone. A horse's two common needs for regular veterinary care are de-worming and teeth floating. Horses pick up worms from eating hay or other feed on the ground around feces. Horses are constantly wormy and need regular worming, without which the worms in their gut consume much of the nutrition that feed should be supplying to the horse. Worm a wormy horse, and the horse will look better in a week or two, much better in a month, and in a few more months as good as a horse that hasn't had a bad case of worms ever or in a long time.

Worming isn't the most pleasant of jobs for vet or handler. The vet must pass a tube down one of the horse's nostrils but into the esophagus and stomach rather than the trachea and lungs. The difference is important. If the vet isn't careful and mistakenly shoves the tube down the wrong pipe, then the liquid worm medicine that the vet next pours in will promptly kill the horse. While feel and angle of the tube can help a vet distinguish, just to be sure, vets listen for gut noises and smell for gut odor as they pass the tube down the esophagus. If they don't hear and smell what they want, then the vet will blow in the tube and then listen for the telltale gurgling response of the gut. Satisfied that the tube is in the right place, the vet will fix a little funnel in the tube's end into which to pour the foul-smelling, worm-killing medicine, and then lift the little funnel as high as the vet can reach, at least above the horse's head, which the horse may out of disgust and pain already be holding as high as possible. Slowly, the funnel drains, following which the vet repeats the process until a quart or so of the medicine has trickled down into the horse's stomach. Some of the foul-smelling medicine inevitably sloshes out of the funnel and down the vet's arm into the vet's sleeve and shirt, a sticky and stinking hazard for any large-animal vet. The hazard is worse when the aggrieved horse jerks its head, sloshing the medicine everywhere down the front and back of the vet. The horse's handler holding a twitch on the horse's nose suffers a similar fate. Get someone else to hold your horse for worming, if possible.

Trainers, breeders, or other horse owners have various paste alternatives to the old vet way of tube deworming. You shove the paste tube deep in the horse's mouth and squeeze, hoping that the paste settles on the horse's tongue or roof of its mouth and works its way down into the stomach. Horses somehow manage to spit out the paste, too often to make the paste method fully reliable. The pastes also don't seem to have the kick that the liquid medicine has for killing a bad case of worms. The better course is thus to have the vet deworm periodically and then use the cheaper and easier paste in between. While improvement in the horse's appearance evidences deworming success, one can also sometimes see piles of the huge worms in the horse's manure shortly after an effective worming of a bad case of worms. Look, it's farming.

You've got a little bit of mess with which to deal. The point is that horses need regular deworming and prosper when you give it to them. All the great food and exercise mean little of one is only feeding the worms, not the horses.

Another unusual veterinary treatment involves floating the horse's teeth. I don't know why they call it *floating*. They should instead call it *grinding* or *filing*, which is what floating entails. Horses gather grass with their big, lovely, pliable lips, and tear it with their big front teeth, which meet rather than overlap like a human's incisors. When a horse is younger, its upper and lower incisors meet roughly in line with one another. As a horse ages, that alignment decreases, the upper and lower incisors gradually jutting forward until the upper and lower teeth together make more of a point than a flat surface. That forward point is a reliable way of telling an aged horse. By contrast, a horse's rear teeth, the molars, which crush grass and hay and, more significantly, grind grain for better digestion, continue to grow as they wear off against one another, except that their growth is uneven where the upper and lower molars don't meet and grind. By the time the horse is about five years old, the unevenly worn molar surfaces can begin to leave painful points and hooks that rub the horse's cheeks as they chew. Their chewing on the uneven molars also gets less efficient, leaving larger, less-digestible grain.

The annual remedy is for a vet to grind back and forth on the tops and sides of the horse's molars with a flat metal rasp. Surprisingly, horses generally don't object to floating (the vet's vigorous grinding back and forth on their molars with the wide rasp) like they object to deworming. Only the rare horse will let a vet shove a tube down its nostril and into its gut without a twitch restraining the horse. Yet most horses require no such restraint for floating. The vet just slides the rasp in the side of the horse's mouth in the natural gap between the incisors and molars and then starts the vigorous back-and-forth rasping. Some horses don't just tolerate floating but seem to love it, like a satisfying brush of the teeth after a long day away from home. Floating doesn't produce the near-immediate improvement that deworming produces but in bad cases can make a significant difference in the horse's condition over some time. Floating's effect is like the effect of deworming. The floating enables the horse to use its molars to crush feed for more-efficient and therefore more-nutritious digestion. Vets also give horses periodic inoculations, especially for tetanus but also for encephalomyelitis and West Nile virus.

The emergency care that vets provide can be many things. As a prior chapter indicates, colic is an especially deadly and scary reason for an emergency vet visit. Vets called to the scene of a horse showing telltale signs of colic, including pacing, sweating, stretching, biting at the sides, and frantic rolling, may try a prompt stomach tube of oil to help ease the passage of whatever is blocking or irritating the horse's intestines. Injected painkillers and sedatives may also help. If colic symptoms persist for more than a few hours or worsen, then the next-step remedy is to try to trailer the horse off to the nearest veterinary school or clinic, of which there are few, capable of performing equine abdominal surgery to untwist the intestines and clear the blockage. The surgery, rarely available under colic's emergency circumstances, is even more rarely successful. And once a horse shows itself prone to colic, colic incidents tend to increase. Colic is a horse owner's nightmare, even with prompt veterinary intervention, often leading to the horse's demise. Every stable has colic incidents. We had one colic demise of a horse that had previously had a successful colic surgery.

Horses have other peculiar emergencies. A horse that exerts itself strenuously before warming up its muscles may have a sudden build-up of lactic acid in the muscles across its hindquarters so severe that the circulatory system cannot carry off the natural acid byproduct of muscle action. In those cases, the horse suddenly can hardly move its bound-up and painful hindquarters. The condition can permanently damage the hindquarter's muscles and cripple a horse if a vet does not promptly inject the horse with an anti-spasm muscle relaxant. I once took a very fit performance horse out of its stall at a layover farm on a long trailer trip. The trailering and stall rest had allowed the horse to store extra sugars and energy in its hindquarters. I led the horse down to what I thought was a shallow pond, got on it bareback, and walked it into the pond. The horse started wading out into the pond but, before I knew it, was swimming with great exertion. I somehow steered it back to shore, only to see that the horse could hardly walk, its hindquarters having seized in the exertion. Fortunately, a vet was on call nearby to give the horse the relaxant remedy so that no long-term harm resulted. The horse had to sit out the event to which we were traveling, though, a significant disappointment.

Vets are also on call for stitching up wounds from horses running into fenceposts or farm equipment, salving and wrapping leg wounds from fence wire, treating allergic reactions to bug bites and unfamiliar bedding, and of course treating various fevers, influenzas, and infections. Disease and infection remedies typically require a regimen of injected antibiotics, meaning that horse owners and trainers get very familiar and comfortable with plunking the large horse needles into the muscle neck of horses. Little membrane-tipped dark bottles of light-colored, foul-smelling antibiotic fill the stable's mini-refrigerator. A stable can feel like a hospital ward when a bad bout of some infectious condition hits, causing coughs and fever among the horses, and interrupting their rigorous training. I didn't mind giving horses shots, but I never got entirely comfortable with drawing blood from a horse's large neck vein.

Where vets truly earn their keep, though, is not with the weekend, evening, or midnight emergency calls but in palpating mares to determine their cycle or confirm their pregnancy. The process requires an equine rectal examination, which is not only messy and smelly but also hazardous. After slipping on a long plastic sleeve, the vet must slide an arm into the mare's rectum, sometimes all the way up to the vet's armpit. You'd think that the mare kicking the vet in protest would be the hazard, which it in part is, despite that the handler will have twitched the mare to discourage any protest. The bigger hazard, though, is different. A mare that suddenly steps sideways with the vet's arm in her up to the armpit flings the vet about like a rag doll. Dislocated shoulders and rotator-cuff tears are a large-animal vet's occupational hazard. One of our most frequently employed vets had a perpetual shoulder problem due to exactly that phenomenon.

As unpleasant as palpating a mare can be, vets do it so often and earn such revenue from it that they grow accustomed to it. The same cannot be said for gelding a colt or stallion, which in comparison to palpating is a relatively rare event. I won't go into the specifics of the procedure because it is worse to observe than you'd think, and you'd probably already be thinking it's pretty awful. The decision to geld a colt or stallion can be momentous. It is certainly irreversible. I never knew a vet to take any pleasure in it. It's probably the point where some vet students decide to go into another career. Vets earn their keep. Being a large-animal vet takes something unusual. God bless them for their education, skill, and commitment. I owed them, as any trainer, breeder, or owner owes them, much.

19

Loss

Skip this chapter, please. As the prior chapter on veterinarians suggests, all is not rosy in horse world. Horses grow old, get injured or sick, and die. They die not only of old age but from colic, laminitis, severe fevers and infections, accidents, and even abuse and neglect. Horses are such magnificent animals, so precious, that every death of a horse is sad. Yet horses can so intertwine themselves in the lives, hopes, and fortunes of their trainers and owners, endear themselves to their trainers and owners, and draw forth their trainers' and owners' care and commitment, that many such deaths are also tragic. The death of certain horses reveals the character of trainer and owner, testing and proving the spirit. Horse deaths also prove the world's brokenness and corruption. Nothing lasts as long as it should in this world. Everything here has the same dust-to-dust destiny, unless one has found the path to embrace the eternal. Heaven holds some glorious horses, one that a most-glorious Savior rides. Earth, meanwhile, fosters some hard stories.

My wife and I lost her beloved gelding Sam to a killing infection, even though when his condition worsened beyond what we could with veterinary help nurse, we took him to a university veterinary hospital for every last effort to save him. We each blame ourselves for Sam's death, although the several other horses that endured exactly what Sam endured all did just fine. My wife and I had taken Sam with us to a string of Florida shows. At the time, it felt like the smartest thing that I could possibly have done because my wife rode Sam joyfully, beautifully, and successfully at each Florida show. Her contentment and success stabilized otherwise rocky performances by our green and only modestly talented show string. But after the shows ended, I made the stupid mistake of driving the horses all the way home from Florida through worsening cold and dampness, chilling the body-clipped and inadequately blanketed Sam in the six-horse van. He undoubtedly caught the fatal bug at the show, and a different infection that he caught at the veterinar hospital may have been the final cause of death, but my misjudgment had as much to do with his demise as anything.

Another especially difficult horse death that I witnessed, although difficult for other reasons, involved a young imported Egyptian stallion that I ground worked a lot, an entire winter, hours upon hours of mind-numbing and finger-freezing circles in the round ring, urging the stallion over higher and higher cavallettis until he was extraordinarily balanced, exquisitely muscled, and very aerobically fit. Given the stallion's birth and early handling at the state stud in Cairo, where report had it that the horses were untouchable treasures but their handlers expendable, the young stallion had been an awful handful when first imported. At first, I rued having to work him for his bad manners and unpredictability, until the steady and arduous work gradually gave him the respect for human sanctity that his early education had failed him. My mentor trainer began riding the stallion in late winter, soon using him as an exhibition horse at a springtime national event before finishing the stallion's park-horse and halter training for a summer show season. The stallion promptly won park and halter championships at several shows, indicative of the horse's beautiful silverfish color, fine features, high-knee-action trot, and incredibly graceful, floating-above-the-air movement.

The stallion would not have been a National Champion at halter but might have done that well in park, if the most inexplicable death hadn't cut short his breakout season. Late that summer, while we were still preparing for the mid-October National Championships, the stallion suddenly died of a brain hemorrhage. He had been standing in the stable's hallway, clipped to a rubber tie outside the tack room, where we had saddled him a hundred times before. The next moment, he was on the cement floor, dead for no apparent reason. My mentor's older son had been saddling the stallion for his father to ride. I was working another horse in the arena at the time but, promptly finishing the workout, saw the immediate aftermath. A stallion at the very prime of his life that minutes before was expecting a vigorous workout, instead lay dead in the hallway. Autopsy suggested a latent circulatory abnormality that would inevitably have killed the stallion, if not then, soon after. One could have understood a fatal accident, maybe an ankle bone broken striking the high cavallettis, or a deadly illness, maybe a fever caught at one of the events and shows. But simply to die because death was the stallion's destiny? The stun of the moment endured beyond the rest of that season, like a hole blown not only in one's hopes and plans but in one's spirit.

Death, though, of which we had sad and tragic others, was not the only loss that we experienced in horse world. The competition, breeding, and training culture changed over time in a way that bred more-striking horses, generated greater buzz, and revealed more-striking performances. Yet those changes also soon cast a frightening pall. The change happened slowly enough that its deleterious effects weren't immediately apparent. But in the end, they were inescapable, omnipresent, constantly unsettling. Unquestionably, investment money, collectible money, Monopoly play money poured into the breed, attracted by a burgeoning auction market. The auctions grew ever more extravagant to entertain ever-more-affluent buyers paying ever-larger prices. As an interested spectator, I attended several of the premier auctions in locations like Scottsdale, Lexington, and Louisville. They were exciting events, with the horses looking their best paraded one at a time across the stages before the eager auction crowd, whipped at times to a fever by the auctioneer, inflated prices, glitzy venues, famous personages, and free-flowing alcohol.

Treating the horses solely or primarily as investments, though, while eliminating their recreational value, changed the calculus. The breed slowly shifted to serve moneyed interests over family interests. The people visiting the farms changed. I had never flown on a private jet before until one came to my last employer's farm to scoop my employer, a syndicate investor, and me up for a quick round-trip visit to the spectacular auction site. The event, planned to impress, was instead deeply troubling, reminding me of an earlier private-jet visit to my employer's farm by a famous (and soon fallen) televangelist, who had surrounded himself by gold-jewelry-draped young women. Just as troubling as the change in clients was the influence that money began to have on training and showing. One new trainer roared to national success with halter horses that followed his every move so intensely that the horses shivered in fright. Other trainers' grooms shared rumors of the treatment that those horses endured to maintain their extreme performances.

Rumors also abounded of cosmetic surgeries performed on the face, throats, and croups of certain strangely exotic-appearing horses who had suddenly appeared in the stable of a wildly successful new trainer. A breaking moment came when a client of that trainer bought an exquisite and extraordinarily gentle two-year-old filly that I was showing to championships, to ship her off to the trainer's stable. I shuddered at the thought of the sensitive filly facing the trainer's rumored methods. The filly didn't have to face much in that she reportedly died a short while after her delivery. Loss is natural. Death is natural. Shame on us, though, when we hasten it, of which we are all at times guilty. I didn't feel any better or more moral than any other trainer. The time simply came when I could no longer endure my participation in Arabian horse world. Fortunately, God paved my way for a sudden exit without regrets, as the next and last chapter indicates. In despair, find hope for the rest and best.

20

Talent

Ultimately, I didn't have any ... talent, that is, or at least not enough of it. Horse world is competitive. To succeed in horse world, you need to be good at what you do, and not just hard working, persevering, and productive but ultimately also skilled, adept, and effective, as in *talented*. You also need talented horse stock. You can't make a silk purse out of a sow's ear, as the saying goes. A talented trainer can improve an average horse a lot, but an average horse can only go so far, and not to the top. Winning requires either an above-average horse in the hands of a talented trainer or a talented horse in the hands of an above-average trainer. Winning regionally or nationally requires an outstanding horse in the hands of an outstanding trainer. Maybe I had the talent but not the horses, or maybe I didn't have the talent. Either way, the realization gradually came to me that I wasn't going to either satisfy my own ambition or provide for my wife in the manner to which I hoped to make her accustomed.

My end as a horse trainer wasn't for lack of trying. Talent of the horse or trainer variety, and likely of any other variety, is an elusive commodity, depending more on what God gave you than on what you can draw from your own designs. Remember your high-school prom king and queen? While they were the talented stars and darlings of their high school class, in most cases classmates outshine them later. Early talent doesn't mean late talent. One can make a great start and yet fizzle out. The awkward klutz in the class soon ends up on the cover of a fashion magazine, while the nerd or outcast ends up a Fortune 500 company's CEO. You see the same thing in horse world: being a great junior rider doesn't mean becoming a talented professional. Having success with one horse or at one time doesn't mean having success again and again. Remember Milli Vanilli among the pantheon of other lost or disgraced one-album wonders? Horse world has plenty of one-hit wonders, too. God does not guarantee anyone's success. His own plans prevail over the plans of men, *every time*—and thank God for that.

The more surprising thing, though, is that one's early scuffling about without showing any promise doesn't mean a lifetime of scuffling. One of the great truths that horse world taught me is that one can start without any hint of talent and yet end up a gifted professional. The indefatigably happy-go-lucky groom Keith was a prime example. Keith, as briefly suggested in a chapter above, was from a great salt-of-the-earth family. His father was a big-hearted police officer and his mom a saint. Keith worked as hard as any of us and with just as much ambition. Yet when his dad came to me one day to ask me if Keith was talented enough to pursue a career as a horse trainer, I worried that I was foolishly trying to avoid crushing dreams or, worse, lying to him out of self-interest when I said yes. Keith's help as a groom was critical to my own limited success, but his help wasn't yet of the talented-horse-trainer type. His help was instead in grooming horses, at which he became a master.

I should have known, though, that Keith was going to succeed far beyond my own wildest dreams, when he started coming to me with training secrets that he was learning at the shows from the best of the best. Using his disarming and joking friendless, a trait that he inherited from his father, together with the sweetness that he inherited from his mother, Keith befriended at the national championships the grooms of the nation's best trainer. While grooms are cooling out and washing horses after a workout and standing around the ring waiting for their trainer to finish with the next horse, they are making other-groom friends from all over the country. Trainers don't share a lot of secrets, but observant grooms eventually discover other trainers' secrets as grooms ply their round-the-clock trade. Keith was among the observant. He even introduced me to some of the grooms who showed me some of the secrets. Keith would go on to win multiple national championships, marry a prominent breeder's daughter with whom he raised a great family, and own and manage beautiful stables in northern and southern climes. Keith had long-run talent.

As to my own end as a horse trainer, my wife and I were fortunate that a very dear horse-training client had for years been looking out for us. A lawyer Mike had been sending horses to me for years to train and show. Mike had a great family. He and his wife Sue were ardent advocates for higher education and graduate education. Their four children, who were just tykes when I was training for Mike, all grew up to go to college and graduate school, their two son's through law school and their two daughters through engineering programs. From when I first met Mike, he would quietly let me know that I should be getting an education beyond high school. He and Sue just had big hearts for young people and their development. Gradually, Mike's advice took root in my stubborn heart. While still working full time managing a large farm and traveling the country showing horses, I started taking night classes at a commuter campus. The studies turned out to be easy for me. I finished a four-year degree at a branch campus of a Big Ten university in just two-and-a-half years, which was fortunate because a little over halfway through when my farm's owner found out, he fired me. Although that firing meant my end in horse world, it was in retrospect exactly the right thing at the right time. An Ivy League law school and a Big Ten law school accepted me shortly later, and off we went, farm dogs and all.

Funny how what goes around comes around. Thirty-five years later, when I was a law school professor and dean, I welcomed Mike's grandson to my campus and taught him law. Mike had sadly passed away from cancer around the time his own kids were entering professions. But his kids had carried on, raising their own children to send off to graduate school and enter professions. Mike's grandson, the one whom I taught law, now practices law with his father (Mike's son) whom I had met a couple of times when he was a child, when Mike brought the family along to a horseshow or we visited Mike's farm. Teaching law to Mike's grandson let me return in a small way the big favor that Mike had shown me in letting me train his horses and much bigger favor he had shown in taking a father's interest in my wife and me personally. Mike, we love you and look forward to joining you soon in heaven.

Although I miss aspects of horse world, I have zero regrets in having left it. My early and middle years in horse world felt richly blessed, mostly because of having met, married, and worked there beside my beautiful, saintly, and Spirit-led wife. Horse world just seemed to favor me for quite a while until suddenly it didn't. Nothing worked. The proverbial brook that fed my wife and I together so consistently just plain dried up. Fortunately, I didn't take my lack of success and reward as due to an irredeemable flaw in me, although surely my redeemable flaws are many, deep, and readily apparent. Instead, my wife, client Mike, and others who cared about me ensured that I saw that my long-run failure in horse world just meant that God had another ministry for my wife and I to share in an entirely different direction. Failure doesn't mean a lack of worth or faith. Indeed, if I had persisted in horse world, then I know that I would have lost everything, likely including my faith. When God points one in a new direction, time to move. Don't look back. Don't hold to the plow. Instead, slaughter the oxen that pull it, and make a sacrifice of them over a fire built from the broken-up plow. Then grasp the new tools that God gives you.

Epilogue

As far as I can tell from modest research, Arabian horse world hasn't changed much since I left it. If anything, the trends that were coalescing then have accelerated in the years after I left. A new breed organization reportedly formed to investigate and police suspicious trainer conduct, to ensure the integrity of competitions, apparently suspended a leading trainer for five years related to allegations of cosmetic enhancement of show horses, if online reports are correct. Yet the trainer still shows, or once again shows, world-beating horses. Values of premier Arabians have further increased, with owners of greater means than ever flying the horses around the world for competitions and breeding. The breed has surely further improved, given breed approval of long-distance artificial insemination, greater-than-ever access to a broader-than-ever gene pool, and increasing emphasis on national and international competitions. Mares no longer need trailer transport, or even overseas flight, to bear the offspring of the world's premier stallions. FedEx air and ground now handle it for you.

I doubt that families have re-entered the breed in greater numbers than the breed lost, although it appears that the rich, famous, and influential find the breed even more intoxicating than previously. Horse world probably just reflects trends in the larger culture. Arabian horse world reflects only a slice of that larger culture, a peculiar slice that the breed's own peculiar characteristics attract. An Arab's primary attraction will always be its refined, spirited, untamed, hot-blooded beauty, not the athletic beauty of a Thoroughbred racehorse, native-plains beauty of the spotted Appaloosa, nor locomotive beauty of the Morgan Horse, but instead an ancient-fine-China beauty that perfectly integrates history and function with aesthetic. We may just be a less egalitarian and more stratified society than we were forty and fifty years ago than we are today. We have more elites and jet setters wielding greater resources to satisfy greater appetites, while fewer middle-income families who can taste of the same earthly fruits.

For my part, I graduated from law school, moved with my wife back to her small hometown, and for a long time operated a law practice before later taking a law-professor and law-dean job at a new local law school. My wife and I had a few good years in law practice together, just as we had worked and shown horses together. She served as a very effective and compassionate legal assistant, giving the law practice the soul that she had once lent to our horse-training adventures. After forty years together, we continue the journey, made joyful by our heavenly destination. Along the way, though, we had a daughter, as one of the stories above indicates. Smart and poised like her mother, our daughter rode and showed only a little, when quite young, and with borrowed horses. She also earned a teaching certificate and law license, both of which she uses elegantly. Horse world isn't her destination, either, but I'm glad that she caught an earthly glimpse of it so that she is ready to enjoy those glorious horses in heaven.

www.ingramcontent.com/pod-product-compliance
Lightning Source LLC
Chambersburg PA
CBHW052033070526
44584CB00016B/2025